WORLD TRAVEL'S BEAUTY

Durime P. Zherka

Gotham Books

30 N Gould St.
Ste. 20820, Sheridan, WY 82801
https://gothambooksinc.com/

Phone: 1 (307) 464-7800

© 2025 *Durime P. Zherka.* All rights reserved.

No part of this book may be reproduced, stored in a retrieval system, or transmitted by any means without the written permission of the author.

Published by Gotham Books (April 23, 2025)

ISBN: 979-8-3484-9386-8 (P)
ISBN: 979-8-3484-9423-0 (E)

Because of the dynamic nature of the Internet, any web addresses or links contained in this book may have changed since publication and may no longer be valid.

The views expressed in this work are solely those of the author and do not necessarily reflect the views of the publisher, and the publisher hereby disclaims any responsibility for them.

CONTENTS

INSPIRATION OF WORLD – TRAVEL'S BEAUTY!..................................... 1

DOLMABAHCE PALACE.. 17

BIG AQUARIUM... 29

EIFFEL TOWER.. 47

"SIENE" RIVER... 53

VERSAILLES... 67

"LOUVRE" MUSEUM.. 91

SAINT ELYSEE!... 107

"LUXEMBOURG" GARDEN!.. 119

"LA DEFENSE" AREA IN PARIS.. 131

WESTFIELD LES QUATRE TEMPS... 135

INSPIRATION OF WORLD – TRAVEL'S BEAUTY!

It is so beautiful, to spend time during sunny day through one wonderful green environment. That day, I decided to enjoy the nature and green environment of my home city Tirana in Albania. The sun's rays were touching my hair, and were doing warm my shoulder.

The sun's rays and sparkle of water fall were creating one beautiful transparent image, in front of one beautiful building that has so many functions like cafeteria restaurants and some games rooms of course ATM and exchange Bank for tourists. Really this building is in heart of center of Tirana.

I saw in that early morning so many enthusiast people that were drinking coffee and were discussing with each other. I thought those people this day looked so happy, maybe and beautiful day was giving to them so much enthusiasm.

I was continuing walking in front of this building and through the beautiful park I got walking to wide side walk aside the wide boulevard of Tirana that is famous for his beauty.It has in two sides very wide sidewalk and green trees.

In distance showed up the big square of Tirana while some interesting buildings like big wide Culture's palace with different architecture and so many new capricious modern high buildings are creating one frame around this square.

The green trees are creating one crown all a round this square. Really Tirana is green city with so many trees and flowers. In this square is standing up the big beautiful statue of national hero "Skenderbeu", while all around are so many important building of ministries with specific architecture that their history is since1930 by Italian architects, those are important for era when they were built.

In center of Tirana there are some very interesting and beautiful building like Mosque, Orthodox Church, that are in harmony with this square. At the moment I saw one big crew of younger people that were speaking loudly with happiness about Lake of Tirana while they were going over there. I decided to go to lake of Tirana between hills. During my walking I was enjoying the loudly conversations of those younger people while I was seeing in two sides of the wide boulevard different buildings with different architecture and so beautiful to the end of boulevard the big white building with stone and white mermer were giving one gloria view to another square in front of the national university with their pride about their beauty.

The road that is with marble to enter to area of the lake surrounded with hills were full with people that were walking and talking and laughing too. through the hill were so many paths with marble that were lied through green trees.

So many names of art 's people, science's people of Albanian and around the world were written to those small roads between trees, and so many names of different activists that contributed to make this park so wonderful. To the top of the hill that was in line with all the others hills appears some monuments of leaders of Albania that contributed to create state of Albania more than one hundred years before and to make solid Albanian language.

Through the trees appeared with all its beauty The big blue lake that is surrounded with so many hills all around. The heavy green space, with blue water of lake and birds of the trees with sun's rays that are trying to discover something between branches of the trees, is creating one peaceful and very beautiful environment in this area.

So many restaurants and cafeteria are aside the lake or under the trees that so many people are enjoying those since early in the morning. It is one magical environment that is giving so much inspiration to people.

While so many students of art were doing painting about environment of the park new forest and lake too. In so many benches that were build with steel decoration and wood everyone will see in metallic label, names of those that were giving donation for benches of for the trees.

I stopped to one student that was exposing three different painting, two were about different environment and one was about one park and aside the park one very beautiful building in Paris, France. We started to discuss about that picture. This younger student explained to me that he was with his co- students of art's major, some days in Paris for their profession to see about art.

His passion and beautiful interpretation, makes me to create my imagination through his speech, while I said to him. I never saw Paris but you are doing me to go straight now over there and we laughed. The student said to me: Absolutely you must to visit Paris, of France.

I discussed with him with happiness I have to do some short trips outside of Albania, in neighbor countries, but I will go to see Paris. I have read and saw so many documentaries but never I was over there. But your passion, your beautiful speech, for Paris made me to visit this beautiful city very soon.

Really, I thought some people has talent to describe in beautiful way with passion something that they like and giving inspiration to people. I was thinking about this younger student with how much passion he was speaking for Paris of France. I left this place of park around the lake and I was thinking for Paris I decided to visit Paris.

So many time I was doing plans to visit different cities in Europe but so many other routine problems plus distance from United States of America that made me to spend more time to my native country Albania, to see my family, my relatives and my friends too, was not giving me so much time to do that.

Like me are so many others, but some times we must to leave something behind or aside, and to see and enjoy some very beautiful, things that are existing in different countries in our Earth planet. Definitely I decided to visit Paris of France.

I performed my trip first to Kosovo, where I saw with great image Prishtina, of course I was to Kosova so many times and specific in Gakovo, but Prishtina, was so proud for its changing so fast in modern way, about high ways so much modern, and so many high new modern buildings.

All around the highway were with modern lights and some streets was so beautiful combination of lights in middle and asides the street. The long highway that was going from enter of Field of Prishtine, through Prishtina and outside this city to connect with other cities, like Lepjan or Ferizaj was very longer highway in two sides with new industrial modern buildings and super modern huge mall of Prishtina.

The other highway like rays were connecting with other cities like Gakovo , historic Prizreni, Peja etc. the most wonderful image appear in Kosovo hills with forest, one magical view of green space, that for me it is one miracle.

Also, so many new towns with modern buildings were creating in Kosovo while I saw in it so many richer villages with big houses modern house red brick, and so beautiful garden around with flowers and fruits. Also, so many agricultures' equipment, like moto-cultivators, small tractors in their garden too, that got my full attention. I thought these people are very hard working.

I had some schedule of travel that year that I was in Albania. So, after I finished visit to Kosovo I did flight to Istanbul Turkey. In Istanbul I was so many times before. Istanbul is much familiar for me, I have my relatives over there plus I lived some times with my husband over there.

As always Istanbul is appeared so much pride with its diversity of beautiful environment. I was enjoyed Istanbul this time with group of friends so my pleasure was more in high level.

From Aksaray, everybody will understand the big history of this very beautiful and richer city in our Earth planet. The famous mosque "Ahmet Sultan", Sophia Mosque, Top Capi Saray, they have suffering two kinds, of weight on their roof and floor.

They have the heavy weight of longer very intrigues and beautiful stories that they have inside them and very heavy weight of thousands of tourists from all around the world that are coming to visit those giant monuments of architecture. From balcony of Top Capi Saray that now is one magnificent museum, appeared so beautiful in distance the sea of Istanbul.

Everybody will imagine so many stories like are alive while the host of museum is explained. Looked that everything is real in all those buildings rooms and environment. Those environments, those super huge building all around with decoration and mermer is witness of the beauty.

Also the jewelry of them is telling for their lavish life at that time and all gifts that they have got by all kings and prince of all around the world

Those is witness to tell people now that and before 500 years before people were working to discover the beautiful nature and to create the beautiful environment and property too for living.

The position of Top Capi Saray it is unimaginable for its beauty and how in that time leaders of this country they were controlling Istanbul in more than three sides of the sea, hills, until to super bridge of Bosphor.

While to the other side close to "Bosphor's bridge, showed up with all its magnificence, another huge very beautiful Saray's building that was used for winter time by Sultans leader of ottomans.

This building is staying alone solid very beautiful aside the sea, looked that it not accepted since that time another rival to this area, while was thinking that was the most beautiful present for Sultan not compare with another building too, in all Istanbul of Turkey.

Close to Top Capi saray is famous "Sultan Ahmet" The construction of the mosque started in August 1609 and finished in 1617 in presence of "Sultan Ahmet" The architect in charge was Sedefkar Mehmet Aga, a student of the great architect Sinan that was mathematician and engineer too.

Architect "Mimar Sinan" originated Albanian man but some weak theories are claiming he to be Armenian and Greek by his family. The Mosque "Sultan Ahmet" is famous about its architecture because in six minarets, in every position everyone will see only one minaret, so much perfect was its construction. Close in this area is the most beautiful "Blue Mosque" that is famous for its architecture and its history too.

To the bottom of the hill of Top Capi Saray, in small distance of those two famous mosques, it is built a long time ago, one huge center with 1000 stores cover under one roof, named "Capalli Carshi". This is big center of business of Istanbul and looked that jewelry of all the world is giving by universe to this center.

When everyone is entering inside " The Capalli Carshi" cannot understand what is color of electric light because the gold 's color it is giving so much impacts inside and looked that all halls and stores are only gold color.

The gold color it is sparkling to everyone and no one can resist that color temptation so everyone wants to enter to every store of jewelry gold. Dominant in this shopping center are absolutely gold jewelry stores after in line are and so many clothes stores, shoes stores art figurine stores, perfume stores, sweets 's stores, leather stores.

All are full with merchandises that in my native country Albania, and all around the Balkan we never can imagined that that were existing this kind of stores and shopping center with super huge merchandises.

The number of visitors and byers are so huge like bees in honey, and needed attention when I was with group friends, because someone can been lost through the way in labyrinths of this super huge center shopping. Diversity of this shopping and welcome for all by owner of the stores of " The Capalli Carshi" it is unimaginable, they have so much patience and with their smile and with their offers for so many other jewelry are doing people to buy something.

The other gate of this shopping center is facing the blue sea. Its position is from place like hill to the beach to the other side. While so many different stores are campaigning this shopping center outside like frame.

While aside the sea so many stores of Doners and so much fresh fishes inside store and outside too that are selling in their equipment with full with ice. Yachts and ships for tourists are in line to start their engine to drive through the "Marmara" sea.

Really Istanbul is surround with water from Bosphorus bridge to Golden Horn. The Bosphorus bridge is 1.5 km or 0,392 miles, and 165 meters height above the Marmara sea.

The "Bosphorus" bridge connect the Sea of Marmara with the Black Sea in the north. We decided to enjoy this driving with ship through this "Marmara" sea.

All people on the ship were so much enthusiast while all of us were enjoying the most beautiful environment in two sides of the water close to The "Bosphorus" bridge where so many huge mansions and palace were hidden it selves under the trees. In the evening I decided to do again this trip with ship through Marmara Sea and I was enjoying the most beautiful view where the lights were sparkling during the night in water while the light of the moon was giving light to all mansions aside the water.

In distance showed with its pride "The Dolmabahce" palace or saray, that its magnificence view aside the water made us to visit it in next day.

DOLMABAHCE PALACE

"Dolmabahce" palace was built by 31 Sultan Abdulmejid between years 1843 – 1856. Construction of this palace costs 5 (five) million Ottoman gold lira or 35 tones gold equivalent with 1, 9 billion gold today (1921).

The sum was approximately one quarter of yearly taxes revenue. This huge expenses brought in 1881 to put financial control of "The sick man European" by European powers. Really this term sick man was used by Nicholas I Tsar of Russian, for empire leader about expenses to tell for their difficult financial situation and state decline.

Sultan Abdulmejid built that palace only for one reason because the "Top Capi" saray where he was living with his family was lacking of contemporary style of luxury, modern, comfort compare with so many others palace of European palace.

Sultan Abdulmejid decided to build with extravagance this very big and beautiful palace in Besiktas where before was another palace named "Besiktash Sahil Palace" that was demolished.

Curiosity is that this palace's project was done by architect Armenian family, by architects: Garabet Balyan, his son Nigogays Balyan, and Evanis Kalfa that was member of Armenian Balyan family of Ottoman court Architects. While Haci Sahit Aga was responsible for construction work.

Family Balyan from Armenia were famous architects and from century 18 and 19, they were building one numerous famous buildings, for Ottoman Empire. "Dolmahbace" palace after its building was home of six Sultans, later. When I was in front of big gate to enter in area of this giant palace, I thought with myself how many histories are in saving in centuries inside of this beautiful palace.

How many love stories or intrigues, how many glories stories about winning in different battles, and how many wonderful gifts and jewelry were enrollment in this palace. One giant tower like gate with so many beautiful color painting from bottom to the top was servicing like main gate.

Between the huge crowd of people that were tourists from all around the world I entered inside the court huge garden to win in time while my friends were coming around with big wondering. Inside the very beautiful garden was another iron gate with very beautiful design in itself, painting with white color so huge so high that gave me big shocking.

While I did one uauauau some tourists were laughing with me and said really it for uauauaua. Before to enter to this beautiful palace it is all around one huge green space garden with very taller and older trees and so many statues. In this garden it was created one very beautiful green design.

I was enjoying this wonderful view while the blue water of the sea was to other side of this palace and looked in some part of iron fence. At that time, I heard the voice of friend of mine that asked me what are you dreaming now?

Really, I am not dreaming but I am thinking how was the life of those people in that time in this giant palace and so beautiful outside. All the others laughed with me. It is right when I see this beautiful environment to start dream for more beautiful things in my life. We were continuing with all others tourists in longer line to enter inside this palace of "Dolmahbace". Entering of this palace was so beautiful with one huge hall and so many huge rooms. The crystals chandeliers were sparkling all around. There were some sections that absolutely was not allowing to take pictures.

This palace has two floors really in some sections was not allowing to enter but the rugs and carpets were super huge and with wonderful design so many colorful. The room of meeting, the room like office of sultan were with original furniture and equipment and supplies, also to others rooms were original furniture too.

One famous rug that was the biggest in Turkey and Europe 150 years was gift by Tsar Nicholas I. The chandeliers were giant because the room had very height. One giant chandelier that was gift by Queen Victoria of United Kingdom, to sultan has 750 lamps and was weighting 4, 5 ton. The host said the history is that this chandelier was paid full by Sultan.

For my observation all chandeliers were so bigger with very weight, so I was not able to make differences of those different chandeliers, all were pure chrystals, all were sparkling and were so beautiful, they were sparkling like diamond.

This "Dolmabahce", palace has the largest collection of Bohemian and Baccarat crystal chandeliers in the world. The price for all of those chandeliers is five million Ottoman gold coins, the current equivalent of 35 (thirty five) tons of gold.

The 205 oil painting were famous super huge with measures, that I got pictures to some of them because permission was with restriction to this section to the other was not allowing

There were so many interruptions, of the longer hall by different stairs that were creating path to go to different sections. There were 46 halls , 285 rooms that we were not able to see for one day, some were closed for really that day. The host was telling to us that are more than 6 (six) hamams, baths and 68 (sixty eight)toilets.

This two-floor palace, covering an area of 45.000 m². The design is a mixture of Baroque, Rococo, Neo-Classic and traditional Ottoman art and culture. Fourteen tons of gold were used to gild the ceilings.

More interesting were some rooms of Sultan women where she was using it to change her dresses in her time, really this room has some small rooms that was difficult to go to see straight her room. Rooms of jewelry was unimaginable but we can not enjoy so much because must to see in distance and to another section was not allowing to enter.

Some balconies and some window of some rooms I enjoyed to see in distance some part of sea 's water, but I did not see the big gate to see the "Marmara" sea by this palace only by outside through the white iron fence.

To see all this giant palace with so beautiful architecture and garden outside, where everything is super huge, like gates, windows, rooms, hall, carpets, rugs, chandeliers made me to think that since that time these people wanted to show their glory of their activity and life and with those symbols.

Leaders Ottomans has great history in centuries about their life and activity art culture and state but more important is that they left witnesses of their life in those huge and so beautiful monuments like palace, mosque, painting, design all around to the wall of buildings, design of iron gates that really has survived in centuries.

From this "Dolmabahce" palace, I got inspiration and I wanted to see and some other historic places of Istanbul and some beautiful modern environments too. Close to Bosphorus strait bridge on the top of very high hill the big antenna looked like was saying to me with its proud:

You cannot leave Istanbul without seeing me. Really, I have see it before but now the local government has done so many improvement to the street and to the top of the hills. To the top of the hill were so many different restaurants and place was full with people , tourists, younger people, families. I thought people like to see every kind beautiful environment if those are on the mountain.

From the top of this very highpoint of hill looked so beautiful Istanbul, with his wonderful image the space between "Bosphorus" bridge, "Marmara" sea until to the other side to "Top Capi Saray".

Really it was one wonderful and spectacular view while antenna has one very modern beautiful shape so high that looked in every corner to the bottom of this very high hill if and faraway to Bosphorus bridge, in two sides close to bridge of the Istanbul Asiatic and European.

Its color metallic is going in full harmony with all green space and multicolor flowers that are around the hill and down until to the main highway. From distance people will see this spectacular view of this famous and pride antenna for its beauty and his height.

It was one miracle to this place to the top of the hills while was so much enthusiasm all around. When the driver of the small bus was driving to the bottom of the hills so many people that were inside make one uauauaua with pleasure for the magnificence view that is appeared in front of us with blue water of "Marmara' sea and famous Bosphorus bridge.

While all the villas aside the highways, and so many beautiful big houses and mansions with different shape with byzantine and modern architecture, with their serenity looked like were showing without noise for the contribute that they gave to this wonderful colorful environments with their trees around and their multicolor flowers in garden and green space all around.

Of course every tourist or citizen in spectacular Istanbul, will see from distance the skepticism of the most beautiful so much elegant metallic color antenna that is not counting those big mansions aside the sea in front of the Bosphorus bridge.

Antenna with its pride looked that is controlling the Bosphorus bridge not to show up for its beauty, but the wind with the birds is sending all the time signal to this capricious antenna that Bosphorus bridge said antenna is taller but I am very longer and so much high above the sea, so we can conquer each other. Another reason is that antenna to be careful because can be skeptical about those mansions but never cannot count the huge famous and beautiful "Dolmabahce" Saray that is not caring for both of us but is showing its pride in front of the Marmara Sea and " Top Capi" Saray , that is controlling in distance and it is dominating high hill with its huge and beautiful building and the Marmara Sea in three angles involving and both of us.

BIG AQUARIUM

Next day we visited with my friends and some other tourists one huge, Aquarium. Really it was so beautiful. This Aquarium had so many sections with so many beautiful and very interesting shape and colors fishes. Measures of fishes was from very small to giant.

The most beautiful color fishes I saw in this aquarium, from gray color black and white, to grey color, with mixer so many colors, simple color like orange, yellow blue open, red, etc.

The most beautiful section of this aquarium was the turtle section, when every body got shocked. Turtles were with different shape with different colors and mixer colors plus were from small until to giant turtle. All got shocked by this section. Very interesting were some very small fishes that were, staying in one dark section with not light.

The interior designer of this Aquarium was so much modern, that made me to turn again from entering gate, to see for the second time, like me and so many other tourists.

I liked all those sections and specific some labyrinth sections that was very difficult to enter to them that were creating like second floor in same floor with others. Also was difficult to get out of those section between glass of those more small aquariums in it.

But I loved the section where so many colorful fishes with different shape and colors were in glass on the wall while those glasses and water with luminescent lamps were creating one blue light color all around.

    Of course it was the section that gave to me so much pleasure with its beauty that multicolor of fishes, creating one harmony with blue light, of course I did picture to this section. The visit to this beautiful aquarium got all our day so, we spent only some times to one modern galleria, shopping center and all the evening we spent to Aksaray that is famous not only for "Capalli Carshi", shopping center but and for so many stores five floors and more, with clothes and golden Jewelry.

In Aksaray' s area in two sides of the main boulevard where is going tramway are so many hotels with different architecture and with different prices too. In this big center of the Istanbul that is really international center of business hotels are for all levels of people label about financial situation, to feel comfortable and to enjoy the beauty of this big city.

Restaurants are in line super modern restaurant and normal restaurant, for all levels of people about their financial situation, that are making possible for people to enjoy the wonderful meal of Istanbul. I loved so much native meal of Istanbul of Turkey, also "Doner" are for me special that never can lose appetite for it.

The Magical Istanbul city, that is surrounded with so many hills 7 (seven hills), has more than 15 million people and last statistic is showing the number of tourists is going more than 17,4 million in year. Istanbul is the big city in all Europe and is ranked in line of big cities in the world.

Istanbul with its beauty is welcome for different people from all around the world. With its price about merchandises and food. Also hotels is making possible that people to make business and to enjoy some beautiful days as vacation with friends and family.

Askaray center is energize day and night by tourists. Istanbul is well known for its Byzantine architecture in different older towns also for new modern town, like Bakirkoy, Jeshilkoy, Kadiqoy, Taksim, Beyoll, Levent, Beshiktash, Zeitin Burnu, etc.

In very beautiful Istanbul is touching each other so many objects and towns and are melting to each other in harmony with byzantine architecture and modern classic architecture that are evidence of their great histories in centuries. So much interesting is the aqueduct wall in Istanbul and Theodosian walls that was built in 1412 to protect "Constinople", so Istanbul has so many mixer history with orthodox and roman empires. Aqueduct wall is with so many gates and separating Istanbul, through this wall in highway can go to Kasim Pasha and all others like Beshiktash, Beyoll, Taksim.

It is creatin one logo – expression for Istanbul that said:

"Istanbul is so beautiful and I will come again."

With those diversities of Istanbul about every things, I got back to my country in Albania, that Summer 2022, to continue vacation because I had restriction time, and this travel was opening the way for new travel to Paris France, before I to go back in beautiful

Fort Lauderdale city that I am naming luxury city about environment, in Florida of the United State of America.

When people are traveling, they are seeing new experience, different tradition different culture and different the way of living so it is not exception for me. So, some of them are giving so much inspiration and some are making to think for others, their way of life, while some are making me to respect what I have and the way that I am living and more important in environment that I am living.

The good and beautiful environment or beautiful city must be for all people to enjoy. So during my trip I am using, my formula, 1- Observation, 2- Taking notes, about information,3 - Comparison, and 4- Inspiration to do something good and great in my life for myself for my family and for others.

It is very important, during trip and visit to very important museums or places that have great history in different countries all around the world, so the host when is explain is doing great job, so writing notes is not allowing or it is not opening the way to brain to forget about some facts.

Comparison with environment of everyone where is living, is creating engine to everyone and to me too, about creating something new, beautiful, idea or vision, in our brain and in our heart that will be used in future.

Istanbul it is one those big city that is giving so much inspiration to people about environment and so many historic objects that since five centuries before, people were working hard to create something very beautiful and esthetic with giant measures and so many art statues that are personification of great leaders and art people like famous painting people, or famous architects at that time.

After turning back to Tirana, my home city that is capital of Albania, I spent some times with my family, relatives and friends, while I was visiting different cities like Durres with its beautiful beach, Korca, this very calm city with so many beautiful private houses that are built by people that have emigrated outside of Albania since 1912.

This area of private houses that lied to the middle and bottom of the hills is giving pride to Korca for their beauty. The houses are in line and between them are roads with stones that are all the time very cleaning. There are some lines of those houses in two side of the stone - road and all the streets between houses are coming up to main boulevard of Korca.

This area is so much characteristic for Korca and is separated by the center of the city. The very beautiful and big Chatedrale it is in center of Korca, while all in long boulevard and to every street there are planted so many trees that are creating one very beautiful green crown of Korca.

So in Korca, everyone will see two image antique and modern city, that are going through in easy way to each other, through their street and boulevard too. While so many beautiful hills are surrounding this city with their trees and new modern houses that have built and arrived to the top of them.

So, I was enjoying this time some days in Korca, with my relatives and some of my friends over there. Korca has hotel for people that before named working class people's hotel, this hotel is on the top of the hill.

Korca is well known for so many artistic events domestic and international with its festivals where so many foreign singers are giving show in this city specific in summer time.

One main and very happy event in Korca is the Beer's holiday in August month that is going three days. So many people are enjoying this holiday of Beer, they are coming from all around Albania also are coming from Greece, Kosovoa , North Macedonia , Montenegro and so many others tourists from different countries of the world. People of Korca are lovely. They love to be with friends during the evening. They are going together in different modern cafeteria or restaurants.

Some people preferred to go to cafeteria or restaurant to modern hotel in center of Korca, but more favorable is one center that named Older Bazaar where are creating to those older buildings different restaurants with meal tradition of Korca, while so much enthusiasm is in that place in the evening by people and tourists, while have music live too.

Also, in boulevard so many people are walking and enjoying the evening specific summer time. During summer time Korca has more fresh weather than other cities of Albania for that reason, is so much preferred by people and tourists too. I was enjoying with full pleasure the time in Korca, during evening with my friends and relatives too.

Korca, is well known for so majority of private houses, all around the city but in center are big buildings. Korca with its district and all villages around has esthetic in green space and in field of agriculture too, also is well known for its textile's plant, glass 's factory with is very beautiful products and precise- metal's factory too.

Korca is city of art, is well known for his theater, for painting, for historic and art museum, and for his specific group of singers with their characteristic songs and music since 100 years before and is heritage this culture by younger people now.

People can enjoyed between others activities in Korca and cinema too. Korca has its University. Korca with all villages around is famous for its different variety of Apples plus others fruits and agriculture is developed in high level

During the winter Korca and its villages around are covered by white snow, also filed , hills and Morava mountain, that is capricious to show itself all around for longer time, but spring season is so much smart, and with it, talent of small warm is starting with delicatesse to melt the snow so the snow to decide by itself to leave the place without wild fighting.

The white snow is seeing the spring time with something jealousy but inside it the snow is thinking, really I enjoyed my time with so many tourists in villages of Dardha and Voskopoje, and in workers' hotel of Korca, also with their skiing, so I am not telling anyway to this lazy spring time.

While the spring time with some colors of its flowers that feel fear by snow are not blooming up yet, is thinking and smiling with its beautiful easy green color and some other color by flowers.

The spring time is whispering with itself: Really I do not understand that the white snow is so quiet for living its place to me because she is strong ally of this wild winter.

The spring time with it smiled whispered: Who cares now it is my time anyway to show up my beauty, with all my bold colors that will sparkle around. I will spread all around the diversity not like white snow only simple white color, no so many people like simple color and same situation all the time by white snow.

People needs vivid color and life, people needs energize and different variety for inspiration, so definitely I am winner with this wild winter and his ally white snow that with mountain gray is not giving so much optimism to people.

The river and lake are turned in ice, during this wild winter time, while the hot sun is shining bright with me and after with my friend, summer too. During my time all birds are coming and twittering with happiness in electric line or in the trees that are showing their green leaves.

On field all sheep, goats, cows, chickens and roosts are coming around and doing noise on fields and are enjoying my time, while people are getting out from their home, since early in the morning to work on the field or everywhere. So definitely I am winner. So with all of those phenomenon and environment Korca is so beautiful. Living in Korca is so beautiful.

I visited Pogradec, that is only one hour distance from Korca, by driving with car. Pogradec that is famous with his big lake that is sharing with North Macedonia. Pogradec, is well known for his beautiful park "Drilon" that is close to lake. This lake is taking water by the river that is coming from Prespa lake, also is connected with other its part of Ohri (Ohrid) lake of North Macedonia.

Drilon, park it is the most beautiful place to spend time for picnic. Everyone will enjoy hiking to area around and hills, will enjoy fishing of trout, carp, and pike, will enjoying boating also riding with bicycle.

Its beauty is astonishing with it spart of water that are creating path for small wood boat, to go around, under the trees, through this park with square 150 ha (hectar).

Drilon, park with green lushes, poplar, its willows trees that are going down until to the ground with their green branches, and so many oak trees that all of those absolutely are creating one tranquility atmosphere and are providing shade during the hot summer month.

This park has so many beautiful birds that with their color and twitter are creating one beautiful mosaic with water noise by boat that are riding around. Drilon is home of "Dalmatian Pelican" or Flamingo. This park is named "Drilon Spring" because of a series of natural spring that bubble from the ground and from lake's water

Through this very beautiful and giant park that is aside the Pogradec ' lake, are built so many cafeterias and restaurants, that people can enjoy during that day. The wonderful view is creating by blue water under the green space of the trees, and so many small wood boat that people are riding around. All around are lamps in beautiful electric tower.

Pogradec, is built aside the lake with so many private houses and so many new modern buildings that all they have red- tile roof that is creating one very beautiful combination of different colors of city. Around the city and to all villages around plantation with apple and other fruits are dominating.

It is created one small rainbow, only with 4- 5 (four to five) colors, by blue water of lake, green space, by trees and plants and multicolor flowers also white wall of building and red roof, while behind them are in line like crown so many hills cover with trees.

Relief of Pogradec is so beautiful has lake also, fields, hills too, also it is in border with small city Struge while close with Struge is and Ohri (Ohrid) city of North Macedonia that are sharing same lake water with Pogradec of Albania.

In this very beautiful national park of Pogradec of Albania everyone can feel serenity and can dream so much. People are enjoying so many events, also theater, cinema and different summer time concerts in this city plus they can visit one museum.

Pogradec has and another touristic village aside lake that is 4 (four) km distance by city of Pogradec, that named Tushemisht. This village is so beautiful aside the Ohrid 's lake and is in border with Saint Naun village of North Maqedonia, but before was part of Albania and was sold during the time of Albania's King Zog to north Macedonia.

The area where the monastery of Saint Naum lies belonged to Albania for a short period from 1912 until June 28, 1925, when Zog of Albania ceded it to Yugoslavia as a result of negotiations between Albania and Yugoslavia and as a gesture of goodwill.

So this was one part of insurance contract who passes the financial obligation for certain potential losses to the insurer that in this case was Albania's King Zog.

Really with Albania are done so many wrong doing about the border and taking out so many parts of its land but this phenomenon was not happing only to Albania but to so many countries around the world that they have problems with their neighbors countries.

So one agreement or document to erase strong conflict it is necessary, one of those element was and about this short time of the monastery, in Saint Naun village.

Sometimes, some leaders in different countries around the Earth Planet, for so many reasons known and unknown are doing accidentally mistake when are selling the most beautiful place, land, village, space water, lake or river part of their country, or are giving like gift to make compensation for their debt.

So Tushemisht like tourist village and so beautiful aside the lake is filling puzzle of the most wonderful panorama of Drilon's park and Pogradec city in south east of Albania. Also in those places during winter time the white snow is covering all around this environment Pogradec city and all villages around, and is doing with its white color rival with the blue water of lake. Tourists that are going to Albania can not leave, without seeing National Drilon Park of Pogradec, also and Albanian people that are traveling in south East of Albania cannot leave without seeing the national Drilon park of Pogradec, because it is attracting with its shinning colorful beauty.

I am passionate for those two cities Korca and Pogradec, because I was visiting most of the time with my parents to see our cousins in my youngest time while during university time this place was my preference with my friends co- students as all other students and specific in spring time that is it one miracle in National Drilon park of Pogradec.

I am privileged because the most beautiful area in West South and East, South of Albania, where are my parents cities and cousins like Korca , Pogradec, and Vlora, with its very beautiful view and famous beach too. So, I visited those cities most of the time for vacation and I know their evolution no any force can separate me from those cities and loving them.

Days were going in wonderful way in Tirana, this summer 2022, while sometimes, I was enjoying Durres city that is so close with Tirana but for other city I have not time were more faraway.

In Durres is starting the street "Via Egnatia" built by Roman empire and this road was going through Durres, was continued to fields lowlands and highlands of Balkan, until to Costandinople.

Durres is the second big city of Albania, after Tirana, with older history life around, 2500 years. Older name was "Dyrrachium" that means, shore, flood, roar waves, difficult rocky -coastline, because the other part of North coast of Durres is with rocks but beautiful environment with so many hills aside the beach that is connected up to north Albania' coast, that has wide sand space.

Durres has one older Amphitheater that has capacity for 20,0000,00 people and is the largest older Amphitheater in Balkan Peninsula. For that older Amphitheater, Albania, has done tentative and claims that this to be in list of "UNESCO" like "World Heritage Site". Durres, has castle that is built in 5th century.

It was my pleasure to visit Durres and to enjoy some beautiful environments of this city, like the center close to the "Adriatic" sea, close to main Sea-Port that has so many cafeteria restaurants, people looked so much happy and energized.

One beautiful square with modern marble where are installment some big supplies for children to play, really this square is so much frequented by children with their parents or their grandparents

The wind that is coming from the "Adriatic" sea, is sending the sounds of the waves to the hills that are staying solid in front of the sea with so many villas through it and so many green spaces, by the trees. So many monuments, and statues are around the city.

Durres city, has the other part of beach in long line with wide space of sand that is continuing to south Albania, with so many modern hotels and so wide sidewalk aside the sand while so many cafeterias, and restaurants are in line. Long beach of Durres is 10 (ten)km.

Behind the main street of this longer beach are in line so many high modern, buildings for residents. This city is so much frequented by so many tourists all around the world and from people all around, of Albania also by Albanian people from Kosovo, North Macedonia and Montenegro.

Durres is well known for its art, for it's museums, the bigger archeologic museum in Albania, that has artifact since 3000 years ago, for it 's theater. Durres has University.

Durres it is big industrial city famous for its for it 's Agriculture Science Institution of studying of illness and bacteria of different plants and protection by them, for National big Sea Port, for Plastic 's Factory, for Tabaco's factory, for its Agriculture Supplies' s Factory, for his Chemistry- products 's Factory.

Durres has so many plantations of vineyard all around hills and fields and to all villages around also so many other agriculture plants are cultivated. Durres has so much transportation too.

The sun of summer time in Tirana was giving so much warm to my heart and was developing and illuminating my thoughts about visiting Paris of France. Really it was July 2022 and so much people were traveling all around so, the price of ticket was so high, anyway I found one good deal about ticket with package with "touristic – guide", to go with one my lady friend and some others in Paris.

The lady to agency in Tirana, said to me: You are lucky that found tickets for Paris, of France, with your friend too, because this time is "hot- pick " -time about tickets if and about 'tour- guide' because people are doing deal so many months before. I laughed and I said to this younger girl, yes I have good luck because I love Paris.

I was traveling this summer so much in different direction to see my relatives in Albania, because a long time, I did not see plus pandemia got so much time that prevented the travel of people everywhere.

One friend of mine said to me: You are spending so much money, with your trips. It is true I said and is expensive all around because life is account but "I want to love and respect my life", after what happened with pandemia, "Covid 19".

Friend of mine laughed loudly and said you are very right, and I want "To love and respect my life", I will come with you and those others people in Paris, while I will come with you in North- West Albania too.

I laughed, while I said, Okay, because I have decided to visit North-West cities of Albania, Shkodra and Lezha. I approved my friend to come with me and another lady friend of mine of University time to North – West, Albania while I said: Do not wait me when I come from the United States of America., to tell you, " To respect and love your life"!

Really transportation all around Albania and to those two cities Shkodra and Lezha, is every one or two hours, all the day so we will use this trip during the day and to go back in Tirana in evening.

But friend of mine did not find ticket for that flight so we did deal to go in North – West Albania, when I will come back from Paris of France. The day that I will travel to Paris strangely came so fast. The flight from Tirana was later in the evening, at 7:30. P.M.

Generally, I feel anxious in some trips but this time I was with my friend lady and some other people from Tirana. Really the plane was full with people and most of them were going with different touristic guide to visit Paris. It was very quiet flight while I was watching from window all the field and hills cover with green space. I saw so good organize the field with agriculture plants in Italy in small measure.

I saw the Alps of Switzerland, but when the plane was going above France 's land, I got shocked that I was seeing so much clear the very beautiful, big parcels of Agriculture with specific geometric figure and so much esthetic.

I loved that big villages have built, houses on the hills, while the other fields were open and cover with agriculture plants. I saw plantation with trees maybe were fruits trees, but when I saw forest on some fields, I made one uauauauau, so beautiful that I got attention of all others around.

Really forest looked heavy with bold dark green while the others field around has more like gold color. Maybe was harvest of the grain because was North of France, and grain is coming more later than in Albania, and to some fields were empty but gold color, so I understood they have finished with those fields about collecting grain. I thought France is doing Agriculture with art.

I told to others people close with our seats, with me and my friend lady, look carefully it is art in their fields. I have worked Agriculture specialist before in Albania but never I saw like that, and we have done beautiful job but I like that. They laughed and started to get pictures really all loved that view.

It was my very good first impression of agriculture of France and their way of systematization of the land and different parcels. At that time, I started to think what beautiful things I will see in Paris.

I have read so much about Paris of France but when I will see, I thought will be more different, because in reading all the time is about writer how talent has to describe in details about different environments of different beautiful cities around of tour Earth planet.

Because I saw so beautiful view of Agriculture, I was sure that I will see so beautiful things in Paris, romantic city of the world. The flight got more than three hours, for me looked that plane was flight not with speed, because I wanted to see Paris without patience.

I was developing my imagination how will look Paris during night. How will look the light of the moon above the "Siena" – river, compare with all other lights and big advertises of the city and above so many bridges. I was thinking about what I have read a long time ago about beautiful Paris.

We entered in Paris by one small airport, that was more than one hour distance by Paris driving. Really, we got the bus that all people were in plane used, the bus for transportation, only some people got car because, they have families in Paris and their children were waiting with their car in airport.

We arrived in airport after 10:P. M. Strangely was coming the evening was not really dark that night. I do not know why I have fiction that the evening was coming more early in Paris never I know that was light until 10: P.M., and some minutes later, maybe 10, (ten) or 20 (twenty) minutes later, really, I got shocked.

Maybe was my weak knowledge, about the time about when is Sunrise or Sunset, in Western Europe. I knew that was more different than in my native country Albania about this phenomenon, but I have fiction is about one hour but never I knew that was two hours and half, or more to come sunset.

Anyway, good or bad this is fact I did not know about this phenomenon and I got shocked. I have learnt that, in high school in general education in "Gimnaz", but maybe I did not give attention to it, more latter.

After we passed control, we were waiting all the others to come in bus, since came all others, the light that was coming weak left its place to dark night, that came with happiness while in her dark gown were sparkling like decoration so many starts.

Some stars, looked small because they were in big distance, that of course were so much faraway, and some more bright big stars, looked that were more closer, with Earth planet.

The beautiful silver moon was opening its light all around, looked that was giving sign to us of big "Welcome". With its light the moon was shining the bold green color of the trees that were aside the highway, and their color looked dark.

Outside was fresh weather, while in two sides of the highway were so much heavy trees that behind them, continuing in distance so many others that were creating like forest. All around green space that I liked that. In this highway did not have so much traffic that night, only some single big trucks were driving in some period time every 15 minutes I saw maybe, only three or four cars.

The night was coming around with full serenity. Really, I loved this night, I said to my friend – lady. Listen me, I lam loving this night with this serenity and I love this environment this is good sign for me that our time in Paris will be wonderful.

It was one beautiful night July 23, 2022, the silver moon was giving light all around and was campaigning us until to hotel. I was seeing from the bus window for bright star, while I said to my friend – lady, I do not see "Procyon" star tonight.

She laughed and said: Maybe you did not tell to "Procyon" star to come out. I said to her, I love "Procyon" start is very bright, and is lucky star for me, I want to spent the most beautiful time in Paris is the first time that I coming here.

We started to make humor while we did not feel how fast we arrived to hotel. In hotel I saw that were so many Albanian people that were living in the United States of America and came to visit Paris in same time with me.

I heard receptionist that said, Oooo, so many people from United States of America. One lady was laughing and said we are Albanian people. He laughed and said Okay so many Albanian – American people tonight in our hotel we laughed.

We did registration and got to our room in second floor. The hotel has done renovation it was so quiet, so much cleaning, so good, so much comfortable.

All around it was one calm situation not noise outside. The hotel where we will stay for four days was with five floors, named "Ibis" – Style. Close with this hotel was another hotel with architecture like Antique, named "Paidcock" hotel.

Close with our "Ibis" "Style" hotel and the other "Paidcock" hotel, while this area was so quiet but some new high buildings started to show up with their new – construction in front of those two hotels. I understood that this area will get developed in future. I loved that place that was so much quiet

I said to my friend here is so much quiet, we do not hear noise outside but we are not hearing noise and inside of hotel this is wondering me. She said: Really is very quiet and so much cleaning about everything. She liked hotel too. Really, I was happy that she liked hotel.

In the morning, at 7:00.A.M. (seven) a clock we went to the first floor where was cafeteria and restaurant too. Breakfast was involved in payment of the room. Everything has for breakfast in this hotel, so many meals has this hotel, olive fruit, orange fruits peach fruits, etc, some kind of cheese of course Franca is famous for different kind of cheese, and I am person of cheese for really.

This restaurant has so different bacons, meatball, soup, tomatoes, cucumbers, so many fruits, peanuts, walnuts, almonds, so many sweets plus coffee, orange soda, so many kind of soda liquid, lemon, tea.

Different kind of bread. We did one big uauauauau. The restaurant and cafeteria were so cleaning and full light glass all around. Tables and chairs brands new furniture. All Albanian tourists showed their pleasure and happiness for this hotel and this environment

The most interesting for me this morning that got my full attention, it was the time when came to this hall to eat breakfast like us, one crew with Asian people adult, men and women, younger boys and girls. They came so much quiet. I was seeing all of them, that they were dressed so much luxury and classic, while women were so much elegant too.

I said to my friends and some to the other tables. Look over there these Asian, people women and men are dressed so luxury and are coming around without noise.

The women that was with her husband to other table close with us laughed so much and said: Do not forget and we before were taking care for our dresses but now we changed.

I asked her: Why we changed? She replies but the time changed and all of us are going simple sportive dresses. I laughed, but why before we used mor luxury dresses and why we did not have so much merchandises as is now, all round Albania. All people, that were listening us and were close with us laughed.

The women that were with her husband continued to laugh and said: but and all tourists are coming simple sportive to Tirana and all around, Albania. I said to her: Okay you think are not going tourists to their country of those Asian people? All we laughed.

We came in famous and beautiful Paris, so I think they love and want to respect Paris that is fashion city too. Also, they are respecting themselves too. Her husband got serious and turned his head to me and said serious:

You are very right. We have two children in Italy our daughter and our son, they are bringing for us so many quality clothes and specific for her, to make happy their mother, because women all the time are behind clothes.

But do you know when I am saying to her wear those that brought our daughter or our son or his wife, she said to me: Okay, next time, I am comfortable, with those that I am wearing daily life.

We all laughed for really. I finished my speech and I said I know that I am right. Now let's go to the bus the driver is waiting us. We all went to the bus that was waiting us in front of the hotel because in 8:00. A.M. (eight) a clock the driver will driver to place as was schedule by the man that was our guide.

Really, he was professor before in Albania but that time he was living in Paris in France, also he told us that he worked and in Albanian Embassy in Paris after changed system in Albania.

He has full knowledge, and was explain with passion everything, also he was proud for his two sons, that have studied for architecture and were working in one big company of Architecture – Engineering in Paris.

When the people came in bus, the driver started engine, so we were starting ours the first day in Paris of France to "Eiffel" tower!

EIFFEL TOWER

First day we visit the "Eiffel" tower. Eiffel tower, is built from 1887-1889. It is named Eiffel in honor of engineer Gustave Eiffel that his company built this iron tower. The Eiffel tower is built in Champ De Marsi in Paris that is one big green space of Paris.

The engineers that created that project were Maurice Koechlin Franco Swiss that was civil engineer and architect also Emile Nouguier, he was French civil engineer and architect too. Eiffel tower is UNESCO World heritage site, it is 330 meters, (1083 Ft.) tall.

The Eiffel tower was named was done by iron to show to the world like symbol of iron culture of France, also has nickname "Iron Lady" About this material iron that was build had so many critics by so many people and artists but anyway they built it.

The "Eiffel" Tower was open for public in 1889 that was "Universal Exposition", or more exact "Paris's Exposition" from May 6, until to October 31, 1889. This was the fifth World's exposition in Paris of France of ten others that is held in this big city between 1855 until 1937.

The "Eiffel" tower is the most famous structure by iron in the world its height is like for one building with 81 floors. This Eiffel tower has attracted more than 32 million visitors, specific the last time in 2015 were visiting Eiffel tower about 6, 91 million people while in 2022, that was that summer that I visited this famous "Eiffel" tower were more than 5, 889 visitors.

This exposition was held at that year to celebrate the 100 anniversaries of the battle of Bastille that marked also was good cause of the beginning of the "French Revolution", that this revolution will change the World in future about social life, human rights creating Republic and so many things.

Another reason of open this Paris's exposition was to stimulate the France's Economy and to pull out of an economic recession. This exposition attracted 61, 722 official exhibitors while 25.000.00 (twenty – five) thousand were from outside of France.

We arrived over there in the morning in 9: A.M. but from the place where was station of the buses was taking time to go to The Eiffel tower so around 10:00 A.M.

We were in front of the grandiose "Iron Lady" the "Eiffel" tower that was waiting us with full smile and full noise by so many people that gave me absolutely full shocking. I never believed that early in the morning I will see one very longer line of people that were waiting between the spaces that were separated with strong textile ribbons.

We must to wait in longer line while for tickets we had bought before time so only to go through this line will take us more than one hour and half. It was morning but was very hot plus so many people and so many noise because some people were doing longer to buy, tickets at that time to the main gate.

Over there were tourists from all around the world of all different ages and so many families with small, teenager or younger children.

Definitely with full patience we arrived to the main gate while we showed our tickets and passed control to machine and entered inside the iron structure. Really, I with my friend – lady and some other of our group were walking to stairs two floors after we got elevator to go the floor of balcony.

Really, I was so much confused because I never imagined that situation, with so many people and so much difficult to enter inside. When I was waiting elevator that was open with skeleton iron, I saw so many people that were traying to enter so fast in elevator without line, without patience.

One man was giving direction and was taking care for elevator was not allowing more than ten people, but people entered more. The man was staying with people in elevator until them to go to floor where was balcony. At least so was tickets until there.

While elevator was going up, I was seeing the other elevator that was full with people and was going to the ground – floor. So I thought those people came very early to see the, "Eiffel" tower.

The balcony was all around the "Eiffel" tower, there were so many people around that were doing registration with video and were taking pictures by their camera.

I was watching Paris that looked wonderful from "Eiffel" tower. Paris looked separated with so many rays of its street for different area and in the middle was one circle square.

Anyone person in this Earth planet if want to enjoy the beautiful view of Paris of France, absolutely, must to go to "Eiffel" tower and to see at least from balcony this spectacular view.

I am not mention for people with jet private or richness plane, but for simple citizens from all around the world, can enjoy this very beautiful image from the most famous iron tower "Eiffel" tower.

Through this big crew and very enthusiast people, I have time to get some pictures and video too. Also, I got some pictures all around the "Eiffel" tower on the ground.

"SIENE" RIVER

In the 1:00 a clock in middle day we went like group to get tour with big boat through "Siene" river. Same situation was over there. The line was so longer while so many boats were waiting in line for tourists.

We got early to this boat like Traget (big ship) and we have opportunity to get seat aside the boat because where so many lines of seat and in middle of the boat. The boat was open.

It was the most beautiful day that the golden Sun's rays were going through the blue water of "Seine" river, while were playing with my eyes. The golden sun's rays were capricious and jealous about me that I was watching with full attention the most beautiful buildings about their architecture and their sculptures in their façade of the wall in two sides of the "Seina " river.

At the moment one younger boy with his fiancé was laughing with me because I was turning my head in two sides of the boat, while he said:

See only this side because we are turning back with this boat in this "Seine" river, close to the other side. I laughed loudly and they both laughed , really they were very good looking and nice couple too.

They both said to me, that they were before with tour of the boat in "Siene" and they were doing what I was doing that day but after they understood that they will see other side too, by boat.

We all laughed and some people that were listening our conversation. So they saved my times and often turning my head in both sides too. I was enjoying with full happiness the view aside the "Siene" river, also I have time to see very carefully the most beautiful classic bridge with their wonderful statues or sculptures.

Some of those sculptures were to the legs of so many bridges and some were to the top of the bridges in middle, some were in four corners of the bridges. Some of them were painting with golden colors.

I think that bridges of Paris of France are one miracles of art. I think and I hope that Paris is big beautiful city of statues of the world. I have this opinion, because other cities have statues but Paris of France has everywhere statues.

Paris has statues on the streets, on fountain, on parks, on the roof of buildings on the facades of the buildings, to every bridge of the "Siene" river.

To one boulevard that I was going with my friend – lady, in break time to see subway of Paris, I saw in long run of boulevard all buildings with statues on roof, aside windows, through the wall, that I got shocked by this view for really. This boulevard I saw again that when we came back from "Saint Elysee" avenue with our bus to go to hotel.

About older subway of Paris, it was for me so much complicated with so many interior ways, that made confused, and I do not know why I had fear to this subway, it was inside very cleaning environment, but so much labyrinths.

I was with my friend – lady. All ways were with letter of alphabet and numbers that giving direction, but I was not concentrated. I used the break time before to go to "Louvre" museum, that day.

At that time, I saw and palace of "Academia National Music", that was so beautiful with classic architecture with some sculpture on the top of the building and some golden color of Angels on the corner of the roof.

Inspiration of The World - Travel's Beauty

So we entered inside subway, really I wanted to take taxi but I was curious of subway, when I saw inside I did not want to go with train in this subway, but my friend said we are going with train in subway. I wanted to find one American bank, in "Saint Elysee" because no one knows to that place.

I stopped one younger boy and asked him for the place of this train in subway, and I said can you campaign us?... and I will pay you because I do not find this way, with my friend we have restriction time.

He laughed loudly he was taller, younger boy, and was student while he said: I do not need to be paid but I will send you to this place while I have the other route he said. He was speaking fluently English but with French accent.

So many people knew English in Paris, when I was asking for that bank, but strangely some of them did not want to speak English, I do not know why? … but really, they did not want to speak that language, when I was pleasing for the place of this bank and I said I am tourist they started to speak very well English.

I said to my friend- lady. They are so much patriot and are fanatic for their French language, she laughed with me. I said do not laugh this is true they love only their French language because they knew very well English language too.

We were walking with this younger boy around more than twenty minutes around and around subway, at last he sent us to correct place where to wait the train. He smiled and gave us instruction, in which station to stop and told the name of the station that will show to train, and left us with one wonderful "Good – Bye".

I said to my friend that Franca has good younger students. After I explained to her that I have traveled with train in subway that are luxury subway in the world in Hollywood Highland and Los Angeles of California where I lived first year in the United States of America.

In that subway was not so much complicated, only in Vermont were so many stairs to go down but I did not see so much labyrinths around an around. We both laughed.

We went to "Saint Elysee" as we followed instruction of the younger boy after I got taxi to go to "Louvre" Museum, while my friend was saying to me let's go with train in subway. I said strict, No, only with taxi. She was continuing to make irony with me and was laughing while asked me:

Why you have fear with subway?

I laughed I said to cover my fear, it is not this reason, it has so many labyrinths, and I felt anxious about that situation. After I said to her with wondering: I cannot imagine if I will live, here in Paris and to travel night in this subway I never will be able to do that.

She started to laugh loudly and said I told you: You are scare by subway, you have fear. I replied to her:

Ooouu, you think whatever you want, maybe are all of those that you are saying, but now I am getting taxi to go in time to "Louvre" to meet our group. So, I got one taxi and we went to "Louvre" Museum for 15 minutes.

So, I was seeing all those sculptures of those bridges and I got as I can pictures, and videos about them. After the boat got turning back to the other side of "Seine" river and I was enjoying with all other people in boat, all famous huge buildings with their beautiful view and different classic architecture.

Inspiration of The World - Travel's Beauty

Those buildings had so many sculptures or statues to their roof, to their facade of wall or in front of them and so many beautiful, green space in front of them too, while so many big trees were all round them.

When we finished this tour to "Seine "river, we got something to eat to some stores that were a lot around the station of the boats where tourists were going, to make tour on the "Siene" river. After we got with group our bus and with my friend – lady, and all others we decided to go to hotel and to close visit of this day with "Eiffel" Tower and tour, with boat to "Siene" river. After my friend said to me: We need to go to eat in restaurant.

I said to her I am not ready now for restaurant, so she decided to go to one store with food and some prepared meal that was close with this hotel. Really hotel was in very quiet place but its position, was not like others hotels in Paris, that are aside the main boulevard and are so many cafeterias, and restaurants around.

This area was more residential area but was in developing about construction with high buildings, two of them were close to our hotel. My, friend – lady, went to this store and bought something to eat.

Really my friend wanted to go out in the evening but I was not sure about that and why the Sun was giving light, until 10:00 (ten): P.M., because subway was faraway and we need to get bus or taxi. I said to my friend:

When we are coming next time in Paris and to get hotel close to boulevard inside center of the city we are going night out. I saw her face that expressed something easy sad, but I smiled and I said: We walked so much today.

So, we were discussing about "Eiffel "tower and tour with boat on "Siena" river, of course I was speaking with full passion that made my friend lady, to laugh loudly while we were watching television too.

It was quiet afternoon and, in the evening, we went to first floor, to cafeteria of hotel to see and to talk for fun with other Albanian, people that we were introduced in this trip guide.

It was fun when one group of Albanian women that were living in Ohio in the United States of America and they have got their family members from Fier, to visit Paris of France, while told us:

"We were yesterday night to one "Disco" here close with area of hotel and we ate over there pizza too, and we danced all the night and made so much fun!'

I asked them: You were not tired by this trip with plane? They answered No. So we enjoyed that night.

At that time, I saw my friend- lady, that said to me in strong way and loudly: You see they were all night out! I laughed with her fast reaction and I justified to her:

They did not tell us that they were going to "Disco". So today if they are going, we will think about that or you will go with them. At that time, they said: Ooohhh today we are something tired, we walked so much to "Eiffel" tower around, plus so many people were over there and so much hot day.

Also, the hot sun above our head to open boat during tour to "Seine" river made us tired. I smiled and I said look, they are very right.

We laughed after. But really that day we were around to "Eiffel" tower, we got up until to fourth floor, with my account because we walked on the stairs until to the second floor and after we went with elevator two floors more where was balcony.

While they are calculating the "Eiffel" tower with different levels with technical term, and after we were on boat around "Seine" river so we were something tired that day.

After we went to our room, I do not know why I loved that room and this quiet situation to this hotel while I was enjoying the sunset later until to 10:P. M. While I was watching television.

I said to my friend - lady: I never believed that is so light with sunset in Paris until 10:00P.M., at night.

VERSAILLES.

The second day we had schedule to go to the most famous place in west of Paris in Versailles.

The driver was driving through this area until he got in one main street inside the Paris, I saw that all the streets has in two sides so much trees, and wide sidewalk that I liked so much.

But when started in line different buildings to show itself with different statues on the wall and to the top of the roof, I shocked. I have read, but I whispered to myself is different what I see with my eyes like physical object.

We started our visit with "Versailles" palaces. It weas about 40 minutes driving far distance from Paris. All street around were full with green trees, all around was beautiful environment, with very beautiful buildings about their architecture.

I thought now I am happy I will see the palaces and the beautiful garden, where is the great story of the younger queen the beautiful Marie- Antoinette and her younger strange husband King Louis XVI, very handsome man.

Versailles.

The most beautiful place in West of Paris capital of France, in in distance (17, 1 km or 10,6 miles) from center of Paris, is Versailles the new town, that was built by king Louis XIV while was de facto for one year capital of kingdom of France more than one century, from 1682 to 1789.

The history is telling that King Louis XIV when he decided to build far away from Paris this new center did not allow anybody to go to see during the construction of this new town or city let say now.

All the construction was leading by specialist and was secret the project while the other people saw this space when it was finished. King Louis XIV, had big vision so he decided to hire three famous architects, one was for project of buildings of Palaces, that was Architect: "Jules Hardouin Mansart, and Louis Le Vau, the Architect of interior designer was "Charles Le Brun", while Architect for design of landscapes was "Andre Le Notre".

After French revolution the Versailles has lost royal status and became prefecture like regional capital of Seine-et Oise department in 1790, later of Yvelines in 1968. Religion roman catholic district. The meaning of Versailles is: To keep turning, turn over and over. (This expression used when is ploughed lands, or cleared lands, (that lands that have been "turned over").

The palaces of Versailles are occupying 9, 5 ha while with all garden around lake, forests are about 800 – 1000 (eight hundred – one thousand) ha that is occupied in this place of Versailles

Palaces of Versailles and all gardens around are UNESCO World Heritage Sites.

The history of Versailles is very older but became in spot to be known by King Louis XIII that got attention of this place that was village at that time, and wanted to build it, since 1632, later he brought to his sons King Louis XIV 3 (three) years old and his brother, over there in 1641 to escape smallpox epidemic.

After in 1651, King Louis XIV came for haunting when he was 13 years old and never left this place but was coming over and over until he established himself with his mother Anne Austrian lady.

Building of Versailles, started in 1669 by those architects about first palaces and projects of the gardens within one years was finished first palace and some of the gardens that they made public for other people to see. Construction continuing until 1710 and later, really totally Versailles got 20 years to be build, to have the most wonderful image that, has today.

Versailles become center of politic of cultures or education and of diplomacy. Versailles is well known for so many Treats like "Treaty of the Paris", to give the end of the "American Revolution", " The Treaty of Versailles" , after the World War I, while today the Congress of France both French, parliament and the National Assembly and the Senate are meeting in Versailles's palace to vote on revision of Constitution.

During this trip, I was thinking about this Versailles's center while I was thinking for the great history of the last Queen consort Marie Antoinette of France before the French revolution.

She was born archduchess of Vienna Austria, daughter of empress Maria Teresa and Emperor Francis I. She was born Maria Antonia Josephe Jeanna after in November 2, 1755 in Vienna, Archduchy of Austria.

She adopted her name in French Maria Antoinette. She married with King Louis XVI in May 16, 1770 in age 14, and she became "Dauphine" of France (wife of the crown prince louis XVI).

In may 10, 1774 her husband Louis XVI got the throne and Marie Antoinette become Queen.

On May 24, 1774 two weeks after death of Louis XV, the king Louis XVI gave to his wife Marie Antoinette a small chateau on the ground of Versailles that had built by his father Louis XV for his mistress Madame De Pompadour.

Her husband King Louis XVI allowed Maria Antoinette his very beautiful wife to renovate this small chateau in her own taste. But later rumors were spreading all around that she had plastered the wall with gold and diamond.

Maria Antoinette, was very beautiful girl she knows very well to read write and speak Italian and French language while German language was difficult for her. She was raised together with her sister Maria Josepha, that was three years older than her but she died later from smallpox in 1767, that gave so much sadness to Maria, she had her brother Joseph II later emperor of Austria.

The father of King Louis XVI the former king Louis XV decided like tutor to prepare "Mathieu Jacques De Vermond", to prepare Mari Antoinette like wife for his son. He found Maria, with very good heart very smart, excellent girl but with lacking in knowledge so must to do so much big job with her.

Another lady helped her to change her fashion of dresses to get French fashion, also to make some repair about her teeth and model of hair, so Queen, Maria Antoinette became so beautiful so much modern but she became so much extravagant about everything about expensive of everything and about so many parties.

About so many things, she became unpopular to French people. When we arrived to Versailles, I was without patience to see specific the most beautiful gardens over there.

In front of us, appeared one super huge square before to entering in front of those huge beautiful palaces that decoration was with gold color all around and so many sculptures on wall on the top of roof everywhere, but the proudest was showing itself one bright golden color metallic, huge with very beautiful design the big gate.

Inside was unbelievable longer hall with so many rooms with different sculptures and big painting and so many decoration on the wall, the magical was the mirror room, with the most beautiful chandeliers.

In Versailles palaces now museum, are more than 60,000.00 art figurine statues and other luxury items

To think for luxury life of those people of monarchy so many centuries before, we cannot imagine without seeing those places. The most beautiful items in those palaces' hall were painting with different measures, but big painting with bright colors looked that everything was alive. Looked that people or event like battle or people in church or indifferent meeting were alive.

To see those palaces with their high level of so many stairs, everybody will think what huge vision had those people before three centuries. Everything was with giant measures. Big square was inside between different buildings. All around, on the façade of the wall of buildings were so many sculptures and statues of people of Angels.

All this situation looked like all sculptors of Earth planet, were gathered to work over there it was very beautiful job it was giant job; it was delicate art in details to every statue.

Inspiration of The World - Travel's Beauty

I was watching in details all around but were so many tourists, super huge number of tourists like big numbers of bees in their, box, that everyone was anxious and curious to see, so some times, some objects I was not able to see close.

It was longer line of people. Also, in those museums of Paris of France, is restriction time to see for one day all those beautiful and giant buildings with everything that they have inside, about art.

To all other museums of France is problem time because those museums are very rich with different things, that some people can find to other countries.

One thing was very important for me at that day the enthusiasm of people about what they were seeing and their high level of interesting to see everything, and more important how they were expressing their big pleasure or wondering or shocking situation or feeling about some unusual things.

Really every time and everywhere, I like the enthusiasm of people that are around me. I feel very comfortable myself in foreign countries when I see enthusiast people around.

Enthusiasm of people is creating inside of me feelings that I am in my home - city or home – country, while cold situation is giving me feelings that I am alone and lost in foreign country or city. It was so much enthusiasm to people they were expressing everything with happiness.

So many were calling each other to go to garden, so I with my friend and our people were going with this crew of people to gardens of Versailles.

We were going through palaces until we found path to go out to gardens, area. When I saw in distance, I shocked I was speechless. I asked our professor. All that green space until over there is of Versailles area.

He said yes all of those are involving in those places only to this center that king created for himself. I screamed: What? But looks are so many hectares. Yes, he said there are so many hectares, after he asked me how much hectares you think are.

I said as specialist of agriculture that I was in Albania I think there are maybe around 100 hectares, he laughed: He said there are 1000 hectares. All green space and all gardens of Versailles that are done with project are 1000 hectares. I asked again: What? What? Yes, he said because all those trees in distance are creating one huge square with forest.

I laughed but I was really shocked while I said with humor: I thought in my life that I was very good Specialist of Agriculture and about measures of the land but I think now it is issue this for me. We laughed. Professor said: Really you were close to measure. I replied what closer I was, I said only one of ten of the squares.1/10 of this green field I never can imagine 1000 ha.

When, I went in front of one concrete balcony with design, while I was seeing the big green design field with one lake in distance, I thought this is one miracle. It was super huge field in this section so beautiful.

I was walking to other section when I saw some labyrinths, created by the green bush like green wall, the most beautiful view, while so many white statues were around and to every corner I imagined:

Pictures of green park with white statues in line.

In those green labyrinths maybe the most beautiful queen consort Maria Antoinette was doing meeting with her admirers or illegal lover as were so many rumors about her.

I thought in those gardens the queen Maria was meeting maybe the handsome man, that she felt in love but her husband that got attention about that situation, send him like ambassador far away in the United States of America, with very smart mind he eliminated one hard time, and dismiss one difficult situation for his position.

I thought maybe when they were close to divorce, beautiful queen Maria was meeting her lover in those garden that were far away from palace, but never divorce happened for so many reasons of empire or monarchy' s establish.

Whatever to be, never happened divorce, plus at that time King Louis XVI understood that that he definitely felt in love with his beautiful wife Maria Antoinette.

When I went to other sections that was full with statues in line, I called my friend and I said come here to see that section while I said to her:

Listen me maybe queen Maria Antoinette came here, to meet her friends that supposed to blame the French monarchy, that others named them enemies of France, but she never accepted that she was dealing with anarchists.

Also supposed that Marie Antoinette, was giving money by France- Treasure, in those gardens in hidden way to her brother Joseph II that came to visit her in France.

Really, she with her husband King XVI met Joseph to another center and big palace in Paris but he came to see Versailles so maybe she gave money in hidden way to those gardens with labyrinth. in Versailles.

My friend – lady said to me, maybe not. I replied why maybe not, she was helping her brother for empire of Austria If I was, I will help my brother, both of us laughed so much.

After I asked her that has one brother like me: Why you will not help your brother to be in richness situation or in big Empire. She laughed. So, Maria Antoinette was very right to help her only one brother and her mother Empress, Mari Theresa.

She was not stealing because she was queen, so she has power to do that. Really, she had difficult time with her mother that she was strict Empress, but their love for each other was unconditional.

After I was walking fast because I wanted to see every section, and I left my friend lady with other people behind. When I went to one section that was one water – fall (fountain) with some sculpture with golden color, some small children with their arrow on bow, in their hand above some flamingo birds, I screamed loudly and I called them to come over there.

Of course, I got picture and video everywhere. I thought absolutely the garden of the Versailles are one miracle of our Earth Planet for their design and for their super huge measure, and super huge number of statues and beautiful sculptures.

I thought when I saw the gardens all around, that "Andre Le Notre" the architect of Landscape that was choose by king louis XIV, is and will be in centuries super famous in future too, about its design of gardens of Versailles.

I thought with my mind for people that are passionate for traveling around the world and those that good financial situation but more important those that have passion, because if they have passion with find resource to realize their trip, if they do not see the Versaille's gardens (Versailles' Jardines) they have see nothing in this world.

In Versailles Garden looked like Universe with its energy positive and with its beauty of rainbow rays of golden sun color of blue - sky color and white clouds color or green Nebula star, has thrown through, the brain and hand of people, all their color.

The universe has thrown those colors to those gardens, to blue water lake of water fall, by blue sky, to white statues, by white cloud, to green trees and bush, by green nebula star, to golden color by sun to the sculptures on the water or to all around buildings.

All those gardens were built with passion and people that were frequenting those were full passion for life and for romantic story. Really when Joseph II Emperor Holy Roman of Austria – Hungary empire,, brother of queen Marie Antoinette came to visit his sister in Paris in France, and to see and Versailles, really he came to establish the situation of his sister with her husband King Louis XVI.

Looked that their situation was cold between each other Queen Marie Antoinette did not care so much for him while he looked cold to her in front of people.

This situation gave strong sign of alarm to Empire of Austria - Hungary, because Geopolitical Alliance of those two countries depended to this marriage, after a longer fighting for seven years that had those two countries in the past.

King Louis XVI and Queen Marie Antoinette, that for eight years they did not have any child that was very important like heir of France, this made the future emperor of Austria – Hungary empire, Joseph II, to think so much about this problem.

He decided to do one longer conversation and if was not so much comfortable for King Louis XVI, about his relationship with his sister Marie Antoinette and about starting child.

Joseph II gave instruction to his brother-in-law, King louis XVI like man about more intimate relationship about sexual details encounter. Joseph II wanted with every condition to keep strong this alliance with every condition.

One child by his sister Marie Antoinette, to King of France Louis XVI, will secure one strong foundation of this alliance, does not matter that French people were not very happy with this marriage of their King Louis XVI with Austrian younger girl.

So, this magnificence view of Versailles, that has cost so much made Joseph II to act to is brother-in-law, King Louis XVI in that manner, maybe and out of rules or ethic of monarchy.

For every action and about everything that he was seeing in France and in Versailles he was writing to his mother empress Holy Roman Mari Theresa, of Austria - Hungary, he was writing every - thing and about relationship of his sister with his brother-in-law.

Strangely the "wild" action, like man of Austria Joseph II, gave great result that soon Marie Antoinette get pregnancy with her first daughter and all other children in line.

This situation changed their distance of this couple so after that King Louis XVI was warmer with his very beautiful wife Mari Antoinette, and the wind of happiness and love entered to their very luxury bedroom.

Inspiration of The World - Travel's Beauty

Because of action of brother Joseph II, the Queen of France Marie Antoinette enjoyed all those beauties of Versailles' palaces, and the most spectacular, beyond imagination of their design and their huge measures of Versailles' green gardens with colorful flowers and white statues or golden sculptures, until to the time of French revolution.

So the theory that one individual with his action can give speed to one phenomenon or can make slow until to stop the phenomenon is so true in this case too, by action of Joseph II.

With his action he saved marriage of his sister Marie Antoinette, with king Louis XVI of France, that after gave heirs of France, and he saved alliance and made more stronger between two empires of France and Austria – Hungary, that this empire has so many other countries involved in it.

It was smart action by him, because he never will leave his sister to lose all those beautiful things and richness situation while she was prepared to go back to her country Austria and to leave her husband King louis XVI of France.

So great people and leader first they put in front of them like priority the goal and well - being of their nation. That was and action of Joseph II.

Who is going to visit Versailles with his wonderful gardens will enter with imagination in history of those people that lived that time and those stories are hidden to those very beautiful Palaces.

Those stories also are hidden to those labyrinths of those wonderful green gardens, and witnesses are those white statues that looked are alive with their expression in features of their face, that is showing great art in details.

All those beautiful objects and green gardens are expressing the love for life and love of romantic story of people that created those. All together like complex in this super huge center of golden Versailles, are giving inspiration to people to create something beautiful in their life for themselves and for others too, also for their city or their country too.

Really love for art in Paris of France is showing itself everywhere on the street on the park on the different buildings with different statues that are decorating their façade until, to the roof with different figures.

While I was leaving those gardens of the Versailles to go to exit gate, I can not stop myself without turning my head all the time to see in distance the beauty of those garden that really Versailles and Paris are proud of those.

I cannot stop without seeing in distance the area with stairs that was going down to the field and was one longer way with one fountain named Latona – Fountain, that service with its water three time in week and has so many golden sculptures around inside the place of the water.

In its fountain is and Latona statue that to honor Latona the god of the sun, and other figures are moon' gods, while in two sides were green space and longer way, that named grand channel, and this project model served and for building architecture of similar view in Washington D.C. of the United States of America.

This "Latona – Fountain" with "Grand Channel" are giving one greatness view in this section of this garden.

All that half day, I was walking around the center of Versailles, through the beautiful palaces and those wonderful green parks with statues and fountain. When we left Versailles schedules was to visit later afternoon "Louvre".

"LOUVRE" MUSEUM.

Really schedule for our group was later after noon so our professor decided to visit the administrative center where was building of court so high and beautiful building and some other administrative buildings too.

When we finished that visit to this area of court building and others, we went in front of this building that really has so much gates, and the man to gate allowed us to enter one hour before because to this gate did not have so much people.

When we entered inside, we must to go through some controls and to show our tickets paper in one very longer line of people. When we passed this corridor of control in front of us appeared one big squares and so many people in it.

While so many of us made one strong uauauaua, we shocked how much people were moving inside building or going outside. We must to drop so many stairs and to go to so many labyrinth halls or corridors.

It was huge building, I think it was not so much easy to go alone over there, without guide person or without map. There were so many very beautiful sections. But longer hall with big paintings and some other with smaller measure it was unimaginable how beautiful and very interesting it is with paintings with their vivid multicolor.

There are more than 35.000.00 art items in "Louvre" museum separated in eight different departments.

To the sections of painting of course I got so many pictures. I think that anyone who is visiting the "Louvre" museum and if never has read any book or material, or never saw any movie about France's Empire or France's revolution, anyone will see those stories to those magnificence paintings, that looked like people are alive.

Inspiration of The World - Travel's Beauty

Inspiration of The World - Travel's Beauty

Inspiration of The World - Travel's Beauty

Inspiration of The World - Travel's Beauty

In those paintings, artists have expression feelings of people at that, in those paintings, artists have expression feelings of people at that time to every event, or in battle or in church or in social life or family. The colors of paintings are so beautiful bold and so much bright time to every event, or in battle or in church or in social life or family. The colors of paintings are so beautiful bold and so much bright.

Those paintings are showing about feelings of French people that so many centuries before, the "Beauty" about everything was part of their life. The "Beauty" showed itself to their dresses, to their buildings to their sculptures or different statues.

Most of all the beauty they showed to their garden, "Jardines" to every big buildings of the Empire like King's buildings and Queen's building "Chateau" to every castles, with their very beautiful decoration on the wall outside and inside, also to other mansion or simple houses.

All those buildings and gardens are witnesses of their inspiration. In every stage of their history different Kings or Queens of France has created something more beautiful than before former King or Queen and so they have created in France with their job this spectacular view in centuries. They have created one big bouquet of different Architecture about buildings, gardens and cities too.

While I was continuing walking in some different section of "Louvre" museum, I went to one section that was like square outside of those halls with so many different sculptures, at that places I lost with my friend-lady and others people, that were going in different sections.

There were so many people - tourists, and so many ways to go, so I was asking in every section different people or some guardians, that were giving me direction to go out, because I thought I am with group I do not need map anyway.

I found the main square, hall and I got exit to other side of this huge building, while in front of me appeared the glass pyramid of "Louvre" museum that is symbols of this museum all around the world with its pictures.

So many younger students were in this aside to this square around this glass pyramid building. I was walking around the building to go in front of the other side where I will meet my group.

I was waiting over there until I saw some of them that were coming from another gate of this building so after we went to the bus to wait all others people, while professor leader of guide was waiting in front of this building to the gate that we entered at the beginning to wait others people to come to the bus.

Really "Louvre " museum, for me, it was not so much easy to walk quiet and to find in easy way to go back outside while so many people are walking around over there. For me it was difficult, because to concentrate to painting and to think not to become confuse to find the way back, it was creating anxious situation for me.

"Louvre" museum it was so beautiful, so interesting and so grandiose, some hours or one day it is not enough to visit and to see quiet and to enjoy every beauty of museum. I thought next time will be good for me to visit again this famous "Louvre" museum for really. That I will do it, to visit this "Louvre" museum again and Versailles too.

After "Louvre "museum we went to see the center of "Saint Elysee" and "Triumph" Tower, (Arc De Triomphe) that was not so far from this place only 15 minutes from "Louvre "museum.

"TRIUMPH" TOWER!

"Triumph" tower is in western of "Champs Elysees, in center of place named "Charles de Gaulle". It was one very wide boulevard with so many beautiful classic high buildings, in two sides of it, with different statues on the façade of buildings.

…While "Triumph" tower was standing proud with is grandiose view and so many sculptures on the facade, of the wall giant sculpture and to the top. In middle, inside of the "Triumph" tower is the tomb of one unknown soldier of the World War I.

Architect of monument of "Triumph" Tower was Jean- Francoise -Therese, (1739 January 21, 1811)

The "Triumph", Tower is honoring the soldiers that fought during French revolution and during the Napoleon Wars.

Really the "Triumph" Tower " Arc De Triomphe "is honoring the success and the victory of the French General Napoleone Bonaparte in battle of "Austerlitz" of Austria Empire, in December 2, 1805, that was one important military engagement of Napoleon.

This battle was named like battle of three Emperors, and is valued by military historians, like the tactical "Masterpiece" of French General Napoleon Bonaparte in this battle of Austerlitz

Were involved 158.000.00 troops and were killed or wounded 24,000.00 troops. Now this place of Austerlitz, is part of Czech Republic (Slavkov U Brna.).

The boulevard where is The" Triumph" Tower, was cover with small marbles or stones, while in two sides were campaigning boulevards with wide sidewalks with so many stores close to them.

So many trees were decorating sidewalks in two sides of boulevard. Really Paris is the city of huge green space. So many trees I saw in every area and the boulevard, that we were going with our bus.

SAINT ELYSEE!

The famous and the most luxury Avenue of Saint Elysee, that is proud for the residence of the president of France, for place Charles de Gaulle and the Arc De Triomphe" (Triumph tower). All huge square and boulevard of "Saint Elysee" is with small branle or stones, with wide sidewalks and so much trees all around, One big historic tower is over there too.

"Saint Elysee" Avenue is famous for so many theaters, opera, cafeterias restaurants and so many beautiful classic buildings that to everyone, people will see so many statues on the façade or to the roof.

This situation will be campaigning from "Saint Elysee' and to other big center of Paris about those kinds of buildings. Looked that the time where those buildings are done was time of the statues and sculptures.

Durime P. Zherika

Inspiration of The World - Travel's Beauty

Inspiration of The World - Travel's Beauty

Really, the schedule to visit Saint Elysee was for the next day, but we were seeing this day because we were going to see the "Triumph", Tower, so we were going through Saint Elysee Avenue and all this center.

We were enjoying all the boulevard close to "Triumph" Tower, all the stores aside the sidewalk and cafeteria, so we were walking careless until came the time to go to the bus and to go to hotel.

When we arrived to one boulevard that was taking to turn to area where was the hotel some people wanted to go to one small restaurant to eat over there. So, we did, we all went to this restaurant to eat later afternoon, but was not lunch and not dinner too, but they serviced us.

In this boulevard was one wide sidewalk in the middle with so many benches in two sides and some small stores for sodas liquid, water or something sweet or hotdogs to eat too. So many people were sitting in those benches and were taking fresh air of this afternoon under the trees with big circle crown.

I loved that situation. So after we ate to this restaurant we stayed about half hour, to this sidewalk and started one wild discussion because in our group were Albanian people that were living in the United States of America, others in Albania, and two younger couples of Albanian people were living in Germany.

All were discussing about Paris of France and couple of Germany were explained for Germany but pressure by Albanian people that were living in the United States of America was so strong so they were winer.

This discussion was continuing wild with loudly voice and inside the bus until we arrived in hotel. Really was one funny situation how was going this wilder conversation, with comment and wild replied by those different groups of Albanian, people.

At that time one older couple said at the end:

Okay we heard all of you and your wild conversation or fighting but all of you were speaking and comparing Paris of France with cities of Germany or cities of the United States of America but no one was comparing with Tirana of Albania, now our question is to all of you:

Are you Albanian people or not?... or we are in wrong bus now this afternoon. All we laughed loudly.

We arrived at hotel and we went right away to our room. We wanted to take rest because we were so much tired, we got shower and lied to the bed while both of us started conversation.

I whispered with myself: Thanks universe that my friend - lady is not doing request now to go out night in center of Paris, while I was watching Television. She saw me and heard something and asked: What are you saying with low voice?

I said to her:

I am watching television and I am reacting. She laughed and said no, I heard, you whispered something not about television's show tell me what is?

I laughed loudly really and I explained to her: Okay listen me: After shower I felt myself very good and really, I do not want to go out of my bed now so I said:

Thanks god that you are not doing request to go out night in center of Paris or to one of center of Paris because Paris has so many centers. I explained word for word my expression to her and I laughed loudly.

She loughed too and said:

First, we are tired today because we moved all around and we were walking a lot, around the place of "The Triumph" Tower and its boulevard.

Second you are scare to go night to Paris. I replied I am not scare because is light, she interrupted me so fast, but is coming night anyway. So, we closed this topic while we were laughing loudly.

After she said: I need coffee I am preparing coffee for both of us. Really, she is drinking so much coffee and she never can interrupt that habit and during travel. I said:

Okay, do it, because I was happy friend of mine was quiet not to go out and wanted to prepare coffee and I will enjoy this coffee in this room with her while I will see television.

At the moment she said I need to go to the first floor to get some small spoon and some small package with sugar. I laughed loudly. I understood she did not like to stay longer in room and wanted one reason to go to the first floor while we were not going out.

Really, I laughed loudly and I said:

I understood you want to move around, but we are going later to the first floor to talk with those Albanian people. She went to the first floor and came back fast in room and brought those packages of sugar. So, we were drinking after some minutes coffee that we tested so good.

I started to discuss about "Versailles" museum and "Louvre" museum.

I never can imagine before that I will see this kind of environment and why I saw so many movies about those and I have read so many things, but to see really original, it is another important matter.

I never thought so many big dimensions of the palaces of Versailles and more important about super huge dimensions of the green space of those parks of Versailles.

I am shocked with all those beauties of those museums and all paintings and luxuries items that they have inside it. Most of all I am wondering for the grandiose job and super beautiful art job that they have done at least more than 250 years before with all those centers and all those beautiful palaces in Versailles and in Paris every, where.

They have started since 1610 but I am saying in majority when was blooming beautiful French, architecture. To think that all those palaces and all sculptures are handmade, while they never had modern, equipment, and supplies for construction, or modern technology like in current time.

Really, architects, artist and construction people at that time, have done perfect job and with so much test about luxury inside of floor or decoration of wall and everything. They have worked with their mind and most of all they have worked for design with their heart with love and full with passion.

This is the key of their success and every beautiful job that survived in centuries, until now that all of us are enjoying while are visiting those centers.

My friend was listening in silence. I said to her:

Today people have so many possibilities, to make beautiful job they have so many modern equipment or supplies but they are not working with passion, if to their private home.

So many are not doing any very beautiful job about decoration of their home outside. I am not saying to make sculptures but some decoration on the sides of the wall will be something different.

More important I do not see in their garden if in Albania or in their Agriculture's parcel beautiful design, that is telling me that is missing their passion for good job only are doing routine job that is it.

In the United States of America, in Los Angeles, in Hollywood Highland, in California, also in Fort Lauderdale, in Miami, in Florida, I saw in different private houses so many beautiful, green design and multicolor flowers' design in garden in front of the houses.

…. While in Albania they forget our beautiful tradition about decoration of front garden of the houses with beautiful design of green space or multicolor flowers. That is not problem of money but is problem of missing passion. If people do not have money for different flowers in their garden they can plant bush green color and to create beautiful design and that is it.

After we finished the coffee, we decided to go to the first floor to the cafeteria of the hotel. It was very cleaning environment and with so many big glasses window for really. We found over there some of Albanian people and those women that were living in the United States of America.

They said that they were tired to go out to enjoy the evening and night in Paris so they decided to stay in hotel. I made with sign to my friend, that meaning was, look they did like us this evening, she smiled.

Same words said and some other couples that were to the other table. We spent that evening to this cafeteria inside the restaurant and after we went to our room. Really this"IBIS" Style hotel was so much quite inside and outside too that I loved that situation.

We went to the room, when I was on bed, I was thinking that tomorrow is the last day that we will be in Paris of France, and those days were going so fast, since we did not have time to think for so many things that we saw because schedule was so much heavy for all those centers to see in short time.

Paris, of France, is so beautiful and those museums need some days to see carefully and specific about very beautiful colorful paintings in both center of "Versailles" museum and "Louvre" museum.

Everything was very beautiful, about different items, furniture, chandeliers, carpet, rugs, building with their gold design, decoration of the wall their interior designer, mirrors, but more and more interesting were famous big colorful paintings and other paintings with different dimension, in two those famous museums. In those paintings people and environment was vivid.

Those paintings needs more time to see very carefully and to enjoy their beauty, but everything it was spectacular.

"LUXEMBOURG" GARDEN!

Next day in the morning we will visit only Luxembourg garden and some parts of Saint Elysee.

"Luxembourg" garden was so beautiful with so many multicolor flowers and so many statues while one big water - fall was in the middle of this square – garden. Close with this Luxembourg garden was the "Luxembourg" palace that Queen Marie De Medici built this palace with her power after death of her husband Henry IV in 1610.

Henry IV was king of Navarra(Community of north Spain by Basque people it is in border of France) since 1572 and after King of France from 1589 until 1610. She was regent to her son Louis XIII.

She bought hotel that was in that place that was owned by Francoise de Luxembourg and wanted to build this palace like the palace in Florence of Italy. She made this place in her own in 1612 and started construction in 1615 and got long time this construction until in 1625.

She put so many paintings and all supplies and equipment that needed in this place, while other interior designer were continuing later. Close with this palace and "Luxembourg" garden was one every beautiful fountain on "Luxembourg" garden that has so many big interesting statues and sculptures.

Fountain's rectangle shape was giving pleasure to people that were sitting in two sides of it and were talking or were reading books while were enjoying fresh air by the water and big trees around.

Inspiration of The World - Travel's Beauty

In this place came to meet use one Albanian lady that was living in Paris that was cousin of my friend – lady. We did some pictures over there and after, that, we went to one cafeteria that was with so many people inside and outside. We spent one hour over there, until to come the time to go with others to the bus and to go back to hotel.

It was longer day but sunset was leaving its place to dark night very later. Those days we saw "Versailles" "Louvre, that day we saw and "Luxembourg" garden too

Everything was beautiful but I think that Paris itself is one museum city, with every his, street, boulevard and buildings everywhere around the city and specific to "Sain Elisee" avenue.

Came the time to got our bus and to go to hotel. When we went to hotel, we were discussing about this center of "Versailles" and I said to my friend lady:

I have read so much about it, I saw so many movies but never I can image to see with these huge measures about every - things. I am wondering with Versailles about its measures, about those huge and beautiful palaces.

I got big shocked, absolutely about those wonderful green parks with their design plus those fountains and statues. It was astonishing view. After we were discussing about "Louvre" museum and "Luxembourg" garden too, while I was doing comment about some paintings that I loved those.

Next day in the morning that really was the last day of visiting Paris in the morning after we ate breakfast to restaurant – cafeteria hotel, we got the bus and all group were going to visit big beautiful church on one high hill Montmartre.

We went to visit the "The Basilica of Sacre Coeur De Montmartre or as named Sacred Heart of Montmartre.

This is a Roman Catholic church and the minor Basilica in Paris. This church is dedicated to the Sacred Heart of Jesus. It is stand up proud in Montmartre high hill 130 (one hundred and thirty) meters or 430 (four hundred and thirty) ft. in Paris of France

The Sacred Heart of Jesus is practiced and well know like Catholic devotion, is symbol of God's boundless and passion love for mankind. This devotion to Christ, is predominantly used, in the Catholic church but is following and by some other Churches like Anglicans and some western rite Orthodox and has begun in century 17 in France.

Really, they are 12 promises of this "Sacred Heart of Jessus" so much popular like those below:

1. I will give them all the graces necessary in their state of life.
2. I will establish peace in their homes.
3. I will comfort them in all their afflictions.
4. I will be their secure refuge during life, and above all, in death.
5. I will bestow abundant blessings upon all their undertakings.
6. Sinners will find in my Heart the source and infinite ocean of mercy.
7. Lukewarm souls shall become fervent.
8. Fervent souls shall quickly mount to high perfection.
9. I will bless every place in which an image of my Heart is exposed and honored.
10. I will give to priests the gift of touching the most hardened hearts.
11. Those who shall promote this devotion shall have their names written in my Heart.
12. I promise you in the excessive mercy of my Heart that my all-powerful love will grant to all those who receive Holy Communion on the First Fridays in nine consecutive months the grace of final perseverance; they shall not die in my disgrace, nor without receiving their sacraments. My divine Heart shall be their safe refuge in this last moment.

Pray must to be nine consecutive days.

Pray is like that:

Divine Jesus, You, have said:

"Ask and you shall receive",

"Seek and you shall find".

"Knock and it shall be opened to you."

Behold me kneeling at Your feet. Filled with a lively faith and confidence in the promises dictated by Your Sacred Heart to Saint Margaret Mary.

I come to ask this favor: (While you can mention your question or request.)

The celebration of the Sacred Heart of Jesus is the third Friday after Pentecost.

"Pentecost" that called Whit Sunday, or WhitSun it is a Christian holiday which is taking place after 49 days so the 50 days after Easter Day.

"Pentecost" is one of the great "Feast: in the eastern Orthodox Church. It is a solemnity in the Roman Rite of the Catholic Church. It is the festival in the Lutheran Churches and a Principal Feast in the Anglican Communion.

This date is depended to the date of the Easter, so the "Pentecost", it is a "moveable Feast. For that reason, the Monday after Pentecost is a legal Holiday in many European, African and Caribbean countries.

For this holy celebration so many Christians all around the world provide a special liturgy.

This very beautiful church by architecture and so big by measure, that stand up on the top of this high hill of Montmartre, was formally approved by National Commission of Patrimony and Architecture as a National Historic Monument on December 2, 2022.

This sacred heart of Jesus is Christian art that is a flaming heart shining by divine light. This sacred heart has part of body like lance wound and is encircled by the crown of thorns while to the top is the cross and bleeding.

In this piece of art in this painting the wounds and crown of thorns expressing the passion of Jesus. The flames expressing the love of Jesus.

The devotion of the Sacred Heart is a devotion of that is outgrowth while believed to be the Christ's sacred humanity. Really the early of devotion is showing that ten centuries of Christianity it is not anything that is telling worship was done to the wounded Heart of Jesus.

The history is telling that around twelfth and thirteenth centuries happen some activities by Bernard of Clairvaux French Catholic and Francis of Assisi, Italian poet and Catholic reforms of the religion, together with Crusaders enthusiast that were return from the" Holy – Land" that gave a rise to devotion specific to the Passion of Jesus Christ and particularly to practices in honor of the Sacred Wounds.

The devotion is especially concerned what the church is giving consideration to be long suffering love and compassion of the Heart of Christ toward Humanity.

Really the popularization of this devotion form, is heritage or derived from Roman Catholic nun from France, Margaret Mary Alacoque, that she said that have learnt devotion from Jesus during a series of apparitions. (The appearance of something remarkable, or unexpected like image of person), to her between 1673 and 1675.

It is another source from the mystical revelation in century 19th, of another Catholic nun in Portugal, who appeared "The Mary of Divine Heart" a religious sister of congregation of the "Good Sheperd" who requested in the name of the Christ that Pope Leo XIII consecrate the entire world to the "Sacred Heart of Jesus"

Really this story is related to one city of Portugal named Fatima and to one of his parts of district to "Cova da Iria" happened this apparition to Marian in 1917.

So, the apparition showed the lady of "Fatima or our lady of the Rosary of Fatima", it was one super natural appearance of three shepherd, children, one was Lucia De Jesus Dos Rosa Santos, and to her cousins, Francisco De Jesus Marto and Jacinta De Jesus Martos.

They declared that they reported three apparitions, of one Angel in village "Valinhos". While in May 13, 1917 in "Covo De Iria" part of the city Fatima, to them appeared six apparitions of "Virgin Blessed Mary".

The children described her like "The Lady more Brilliant than the Sun", also the children said the pray will help to end the great war that time was the World War I.

Also, they explained that "Virgin Blessed Mary" will appear in October 13, 1917, she will reveal her identity and will perform some miracles. She told them to pray in June 13, 1917 for Rosary daily for miracle. So, between May 13, and October 13, children saw six apparitions.

Those apparitions, told to them and about other Global War on Earth planet as it was World War II, and possibility of other Global Wars in future, also, about Consecration of Russia to the Immaculate "Heart of Mary, and about and some others phenomenon, like "Miracle of the Sun".

Jose Alveas Corriea De Silva, Bishop of Leiria declared the event worthy of beliefs on October 13, 1930, since that time in Portugal are so many rituals that starting for Lady Fatima since May 13, every year that so many pilgrims are going over there to do that ritual or pray for Rosary.

Virgin blessed Mary was the first century Jewish woman of Nazareth, the wife of Joseph and the mother of Jesus.

She is main figure of Christianity, also she has so many title like Queen, or Litany of Loreto.

So many churches, of the Eastern and Oriental Orthodox also church of the East, Catholic, Anglican and Lutheran churches believe that Mary is mother of Jesus is the "Mother of the God"

She has the highest position in Islam too, of all the women and is mentioned numerous times in the Quran.

Those facts are telling for sacrifice or devotion of humanity and for helping that is coming by pray in the name of Saint figures on Earth planet.

Also, this Sacre- Coeur Basilica is built, to the top of this hill and his 200 (two hundred) meters above the Seine river, it so bigger with so beautiful image and architecture, from its point it is overlooks the entire Paris city and its suburbs. This Sacre – Coeur Basilica, of the "Sacred Heart of Jesus", is the second most popular tourist destination after The Eiffel Tower in Paris of France.

After we visited this Basilic where the line of people was so longer, and I got picture over there we went to one cafeteria aside the boulevard. To the boulevard and wide sidewalk in middle of boulevard were so many people that were waiting to visit this basilic.

After cafeteria we got the bus and all of us were going to visit the area of "La Defense" area in Paris.

"LA DEFENSE" AREA IN PARIS.

"La Defense" is new modern town and it is center of business district of Paris, of France is metropolitan area. It is 3 kilometers (three) (1,9 mi) West of the city limit. It is the largest center of business in Europe, with 560 (five hundred and sixty) hectares, or 1400 (one thousand and four hundred) acres, they are working daily life about 180,000 workers.

In this super modern business center are about 72 (seventy two) glass and steel buildings, skyscrapers which 20 buildings are completed out of 24 others in Paris region.

In this center or new modern city let's name it are 3, 500.000 (three million and five hundred) meters, or (38.000.000 square ft) (thirtyeight million) sq/ft for office space. It is lied in four communes of Paris like Courbevoie, La Garenne - Colombos, Nanterre, and Puteaux. Also, it is located in LLE -De France region's department of Hauts- de Siene.

When we arrived over there the professor was speaking so much enthusiast and full with passion, I was watching carefully but I did not expression any feeling this time.

He saw me, when he finished his speech came close to me. I was with some women one adult couple and my friend - lady. We were in middle of one very big square all cover with marbles and one very high modern glass building, "EDF", Corp. was in front of us , another very high modern glass building of energetic and all others in line.

He asked me: You did not got impression by those buildings by this very modern and beautiful center. I was seeing him and I did not want to put in low level his passion of explanation and he liked this center, but I said to him with smile:

Do you want the true answer by me? Yes, he said tell me the true.

It is so much modern this new city let's say is so beautiful but I did not have impression. At that moment I said loudly:

Ah Paris, Paris! They all laughed. I explained to him: I saw Gratacels, very high buildings in the United States of America, and those are grandiose super modern and very beautiful glass buildings, so high, but looked that are so close with each other.

So they are making my eyes to work hard to see their specific architecture of each other, because as you see are not the same. While this center looked small that this square is so bigger because of those very close and very high buildings.

They started to discuss with each other and I said first I am going to see that building that is like arch. It was one very high building, like shape of "Triumph" tower but it was higher and bigger and with modern architecture not classic.

I said to our leader professor I want to go to see that building. He told me the name of it "Grande Arche. I went over there and I got some pictures of this building in distance.

It was super modern. I did not have time to come around it because I did not want to lose my crew of people. After I was seeing in line all those buildings that were in front of me.

While we were walking to so many stairs and went to see to one shopping centers that were new stores and cafeteria. We came around those small stores outside after, we entered to one modern bigger cafeteria that was servicing and some food. It was so beautiful inside and modern furniture inside. I loved that place, it was very cleaning, while younger people that were servicing to computer cash front and others were very helpful all were younger and knew English very well, so we did not have any problem to talk with them.

For me was good because I was seeing from the front windows that were bigger and glass, I was enjoying again in quiet way all those very modern high glass skyscraper buildings in front of me. I spent more time inside this cafeteria while the others were coming around to some small stores or modern boutiques.

I loved that image for really and I felt myself peaceful. My friend was coming all around to different stores that were in same building of cafeteria in line outside.

One younger girl that was servicing to this modern cafeteria came to give me the password of internet and she asked me:

You do not want to see the stores outside with your friends?, really all they were out but their bags were inside of the cafeteria because those younger people said go see out, it is not about bags, not problem nobody will touch.

She explained to me do not think for your bag leave here if you want to see outside stores. I said:

I do not have problem but I saw the stores all around before to enter here in cafeteria, also I like this view of those buildings in front of me though big glass window I feel that I am outside and we laughed.

She asked me where I come from I explained to her I am with vacation in Albania and current time here in Paris in your beautiful Paris, of France, but I am living in Fort Lauderdale, of Florida of the United States of America.

She laughed and said to me:

Aaahhhaaa: For this reason, you are not going to see those stores. I replied to her. No it is not this reason, because after we are going to Galleria that is to the other gate in small distance of this building and we will eat again over there and I will see about any items to buy from Paris.

Did you like merchandise in Paris, she asked me? I answered fast I liked some of them but I did not like price. I saw so many golden jewelry, that I liked to buy to "Cartier" store were so much expensive.

Definitely I said to her with smile Paris, is so much expensive what I saw until now, let's see in Galleria now what is I said to her. She laughed and said for Americans are not problem price of Paris.

I replied to her very fast, American people are not finding money on the street, nobody is throwing money outside for others. It is hard job earning money in the United States of America, so I do not know how easy is job in France and specific in Paris, but I am telling you here it is very expensive.

She smiled and told me that she was student and was working too. I said good for you. I told her:

…And I studied and worked in the United States of America and why I had University from my country so it is very good for you to study and to get job that you want and to something beautiful like those buildings for Paris and France your country. I think everyone must to work every kind of job just to work, and study, because the better is coming. She said:

Thank You, and laughed, she was very younger and so much simpatico.

After one hour we left this cafeteria and all younger people that were working over there, were happy with all our crew, because we made so much jokes with them, after that we went to Galleria.

WESTFIELD LES QUATRE TEMPS.

Westfield, Les Quatre Temps, super modern glass building architecture with so many stairs in front of it and so many gates to enter or to exit, to other sides of building, appear proud for its beauty in company of those very high glass building.

Really for its function was more attractive for people that wanted to enter over there from all around the world that those high capricious building that wanted to show up that were more important that Galleria.

The very high glass modern buildings, were thinking that are more important, than galleria, because they were closer to the sky to the Golden Sun during the day, and Silver Moon during the night.

…While they were greeting the Golden Sun during the day with turning back of his rays by their glasses while Silver Moon were greeting night with their lights of their office so they want to ensure those two allies that loves them.

They greeting them all the time day and night, because, anyway they need for their business, the energy of the Sun and Stellar energy of stars that are close with Silver Moon during night.

…But Westfield Galleria has it pride for so many stores, because this galleria is home of more than 220 (Two hundred twenty) stores, 48 (forty eight) restaurants, and 24 screen movie theater. This galleria is the largest shopping center in "La Defense" town really it become new modern city with its dimension

When we entered to this modern huge galleria one adult lady wanted to go to find the restroom also, she wanted to make and clean her hands and face with water.

She found it in that longer hall and came fast to tell to some of us that were together: Oooo my God ooohhh my God, who has exchange Euro, because to enter inside in rest room if to wash face and hand is with euro.

I said loudly Aaaahhh, America, America. Aaahhh U.S.A. U.S.A. all laughed loudly, and some adult Albanian women that were living in Ohio of the United States of America laughed loudly and said now we see what is the difference between United States of America and France and famous Paris.

Galleria was so modern, with so many decoration inside , very bigger, all different corporations of retails that are in the United States of America I saw over there, in some stores price were normal like in the United States of America while some were so much expensive.

Jewelry golden with diamond or silver absolutely very expensive were and to Galleria. Really, I was seeing for fun because I bought in Istanbul of Turkey, that summer some gold jewelry.

Istanbul of Turkey, It is in my heart about golden and diamond Jewelry and Zales Inc's store of diamond, gold and silver in the United States of America. I am loyal member to them in Istanbul and in Zales.

Zales store, (Zales Corp.) about her business has so many beautiful items and very beautiful and elegant design of Jewelry, it is my favorite store and company too.

We were going all around this modern Galleria in all her floors and were spending good times sometimes, we were sitting to the luxury benches that were aside like balcony to upper floor and were seeing all stores and people around. It was funny situation. I loved that enthusiasm of the people to Galleria.

The new modern town "La Defense" has name after the statues of "La Defense" de Paris, by Louis – Ernest Barrias, which was built to honor and to show respect for the soldiers who had defended Paris during the Franco- Prussian War.

About, "La Defense", the Public Establishment decide to start this new modern town with super modern glass buildings, while began to slowly replace the city's factories, and a few farms. The first building was" Esso Tower" in 1958 the center of New Industries and Technologies (CNIT) was built and first used.

"La Defense" is town of so many big headquarters of big corporations like

"Societe Generale", " Neuf Cegetel" "Total Energies" with super modern high glass building was showing itself so much proud in front of this big square. "EDF with wonderful giant glass building, "RTE", "Aventis", "Areva" Arcelor, also "Westfield les for Temps", all those glass modern high buildings were doing rivals with each other.

The first line of buildings or first generation, building skyscraper that all were similar about their appearance about 100 (one hundred) meters high or 330 (three hundred thirty) ft.

While in 1966 was built the first high skyscraper building for business office that named "Nobel" Tower. In 1970 was opened the "RER" line a railway from "La Defense" to "Etoile". In 1974 was done one contract for high speed, train but after was cancel was abandoned.

In 1970 was rising demand for residences and offices in this new area so started the second generation of new modern glass skyscraper buildings so many new buildings were appear around, while one economic crisis stopped this developing of construction.

In 1980 started the third generation of those glass modern high building also was started building the big shopping center in Europe at that time named " "The Quatre Temps" in 1981.

In 1990 one big project was by "Management and Development Office" about one big concert the Tete Defense Bastille Day that was held to big high building "Grande Arche and to three' are towers about projection screen and one building pyramidal stage above the road. That concert was composed by French electronic Jean – Michel Jarre in this square between those buildings

To this free concert titled "Paris La Defense" attracted 2 (Two) million spectators that their lines was extending until to "Triumph" Tower or the " Arc De Triomphe.) this was the largest World concert at that time in Paris.

In 1997 French Jean – Michel Jarre, German DJ Sash, and the singer La Tres, prepared one videoclip with their song " Stay at LA Defense".

During this time so many modern hotels started to build in new modern , "La Defense" while in 1992 the Line 1, of Paris - Metro was extended to "La Defense" that made so much accessible this city.

"La Defense" new town is the big business center in Europe where are established the bigger corporations of the Paris of France with so many urbans are in Paris. This town has 50.000.00 (Fifty thousand) permanent residents and 75.000.00 (seventy five, thousand) students.

This new town La Defense that is going in future to become new modern glass city is in western of the "Historical Axis" of Paris in 10 (ten) kilometer or

6.2 mi.

"Historical Axis" or "Axe Historique" of Paris extended those area, it is starting with "Louvre "museum in central Paris, continues to Champs- Elysees, to "Triumph" Tower, is going along the avenue "De La Grande Armee" before to meet to "La Defense" new modern town.

"La Defense" visited by 8.000.000.00 (eight million) tourists each year and is open museums too.

In December 2005 The Management of Development Office creating one aggressive project for nine years that named "La Defense 2006 - 2015 to build so many buildings, to create balance of buildings of office and residential houses, also to improve in high level transportation of local employees from their home to "La Defense" easier.

"La Defense" was so modern with so beautiful glass buildings, with big Galleria with big square in front of those buildings, and so many buses has big station to this center of business district, also had so many tourists that was futurist town and very different from older classical Paris.

About older classical Paris of France, I was speechless, about everything. Older classic Paris is remarkable, about everything, about "Eiffel Tower, every bridges to "Siene" river, of all boulevards and streets to center of Paris and "Saint Elysee", and their buildings in two sides decorated with sculptures.

… Aso "Luxembourg"- garden, "Triumph" Tower and Grandiose Louvre" museum and wonderful "Versailles" with its beautiful palaces and magnificence green garden and parks too, are doing so beautiful this line like one older diamond necklace in chest of Paris of France.

La Defense town is giving importance education, and have "Leonardo Da Vinci "University, IA institute, four different Business school like, EDC,(Paris Business School), ESSEC, (Business School), ICN, (Graduate Business School), IESEG " School of Management).

"La Defense" town, has European Paris – La Defense an internationally, primary, and secondary school that was accredited in 2020 like European school.

So this new town it is one big opportunity for children pupils and students to be prepared for all around the Europe with their professional major.

For my impression what I saw in this center of "La Defense" town, I can not imagined that was so bigger town. It looked that all the glass high buildings were collected around this square center, in front of building of EDF, Total Energies", Galleria - Westfield and Grand arche Buildings and so many others buildings close around.

We did not have time to go so much around but "La Defense"modern glass town, it is very important for ingredient that it has inside it, like so many powerful business corporations, so many European and French schools for education and so big shopping center and high level of transportation.

My travel to Paris was something that I never can imagined that I will see so many wonderful things. This visit I must have done so many years before since I am living in the United States of America, because before in Albania we did not have alternative to go out of the world and to make tourism.

But to visit Paris is like to get education about architecture, about art, about design of silviculture of landscape. Paris like beautiful and big city with two different environments classical and futurist modern is giving so much inspiration to people for life and about developing of creative job.

Life in Paris was so much with enthusiasm, so much with energies, everywhere and every time. Classical and futurist modern architecture in Paris of France was in harmony with green and colorful environment all around and modern infrastructure too.

To visit Paris of France means to create very beautiful memories of a beautiful time in this big, romantic and very beautiful city.

To visit modern, futurist, and new "La Defense" area town of Paris of France, with so many modern high buildings it is addition of one more worth gemstone in memories. At the evening, we will travel by plane to go back to Albania.

When I finished this travel, I was happy for my new experience that I had, for so many beautiful and interesting things that I saw. After those really three trips, to Kosovo, Istanbul of Turkey and Paris of France, I made addition some more beautiful original pearl not cultivate pearl to my longer necklace of memories.

I think in future to create another longer necklace with different worth color gemstones like all different color of Diamond, Saphire, Rubin, Aquamarine, Amethyst, Agata, Zircon etc, of beautiful memories.

When I travel my priority, is to see as much as I can and how much I am able to do, because depended by time and by financial situation, so I like to see environment beautiful part of city and some museums that I can afford because ticket of museum it is something to be in consideration.

Also, the museums to get in consideration that to put more reasonable price. I was seeing this phenomenon in Istanbul so many people cannot go to see museum because of the high payment of ticket.

During my trip I am happy because I see different tradition, different culture and different kind of meal on restaurants. I am not concentrated to buy so many things but I have created and follow one routine to by one item, that is symbol of the country that I visit, while for the other things I am very careful about the price how much will cost.

During my travel I meet new people, I can hear new stories, I can hear their experience about their travel too, that is preparing me for other trip too, for different country.

I like to travel that does not mean big or less amount of money or about my financial situation this matter has to do with my courage to create conditions so, I can perform travel that I want.

When I decide to travel, I will do search about the time of the year that I can find good ticket for my pocket that I can afford with all other expenses.

During my trip to different countries, by instinct my brain is going to my current country in Florida of the United States of America, that I live, and to my native country Albania, that I have lived, and I see so many different situations, and specific for Albania.

My travel is giving to me so much inspiration for new great things, that to discuss and to create, also is giving my courage to express my opinion for something that needed to change.

Also the travel is giving me so much enthusiasm about story teller because the, travel is making me rich by new ideas and knowledge not rich by things like clothes shoes or jewelry.

So, when I am doing one trip my mind is working hard in future time to explore another country to visit. In this way I am so much optimist to convince mind of my relatives, or friends, to travel not to stay constant in one place.

All the time that I am traveling I am making addition in my memories something new that will be with me in my mind for so longer, so when I am going back to my home, I am quite to think so much and to remember what I saw during this travel.

Travel to new country with its diversity is changing me about some points of concept of life, also is making me to discover about myself, what I like in my life and what I am for really by myself.

When I see different standard, of life and the way of other people living that is creating me another concept how is depended their living and standard life about their environment.

This situation is making me more sensible and compassionate about people, and is making me happy for what I have in my normal life, by my job. ...While to say Thank

You to Universe for creating possibility for my normal life and about traveling that is one privilege for me and for everyone that is traveling.

People that are not traveling in their life never they can see the difference of life in different countries and maybe they will be not able to appreciate what they have.

I think that World is full of surprises, as I saw "The Dolmabahce" museum in Istanbul Turkey, "Versailles" and "Louvre" museum and "Saint Elysee" avenue and center, that all of those left me speechless for really.

Everyone can get so many information and knowledge in different travels

After we finished visiting some part of "La Defense" new town of Paris of France, walked and dropped some stairs to go from this square to the street where was bus's station and our bus, where the driver was waiting for all our crew of people.

This station was between all those glass buildings and the Grande Arche building too. The driver started engine while I was seeing around La Defense until the bus got out to the highway to go to same Airport that we came some days before.

I was enjoying the evening through the highway that was full with trees on two sides until to airport. When we arrived to airport was a longer line of people. After we passed control we were waiting the time to get inside the plane, while, we were discussing with each other about those museums.

Came the time to enter in plane, I got seat and I was seeing outside, until the plane to start its flying. At the moment that aircraft started it engine I said now I left the beautiful romantic city of Paris.

During time of flying, the night with its decoration by so many stars was spreading quietly its dark color all around the sky. In distance appeared the beautiful silver moon that was creating slowly it's circle shape of it's body and was giving strong light all around.

The Procyon Star was giving it's bright shine ray through the window of the plane to my eyes, looked that all of those stars were greeting me with happiness for my travel in Paris.

In distance I saw one figure with orange color intervene to lily, color, a little blue color, and red color to the end. I thought, right away were coming up the sky four very beautiful Nebula stars.

The orange color Nebula star, showed more bigger that body while others looked like were keeping low profile to give greeting to me, maybe they were careful, by the Procyon star that wanted to dominate that night with its light divine shinning.

Looked that they said to me: We are happy that you visited those museums and this city and we saw for really how much positive energy we gave to people of Earth planet to do the great and wonderful job.

We are grateful that those people gave big, Thank You, to us with their different art figures and sculpture of Angels that are in our divine cosmic area.

You saw our Golden Sun, the beautiful Silver Moon, and brightest Stars, to their painting too, in this beautiful city of Paris of France, and to the other magnificence city of Istanbul of Turkey , everywhere we were present on their art beautiful job.

You got one big and beautiful experience of art and older classical architecture and modern architecture too. You saw so many beautiful green spaces of garden and colorful garden too, that those people used the divine colors, of our rainbow.

You must to understand that our positive energy was so much efficiency to those people that have created so many wonderful things during their life and for their life.

We have decided to give you so much positive energy by all our brightest stars, like Procyon star, all Deneb stars like crew, Sirius star, Vega star, both Major and Minor Ursa stars, all colorful Nebula stars, Orion Star, Andromeda star, also we have decided to create one big privilege for you to give strong positive energy and by Antares star that is red hued star like Mars.

In this way we are helping you to have full positive energy and full inspiration and to do another travel to another country or other countries and to write for those countries and for us too and good luck about this travel in future.

I whispered: Thank you my dearest stars for your positive energy and for another opportunity, for another new travel and I closed in gentle way the cover of the aircraft's window while I was waiting to arrive in Tirana of Albania.